A HANDBOOK OF
ENGLISH MEDIEVAL SCULPTURE

WELLS CATHEDRAL

West Front

A Handbook of
ENGLISH MEDIEVAL SCULPTURE

by

ARTHUR GARDNER

M.A., F.S.A.

NEW YORK: THE MACMILLAN COMPANY
CAMBRIDGE, ENGLAND: AT THE UNIVERSITY PRESS
1937

LONDON
Cambridge University Press
FETTER LANE

NEW YORK · TORONTO
BOMBAY · CALCUTTA · MADRAS
Macmillan

TOKYO
Maruzen Company Ltd

First Edition 1935
Reprinted 1937

PREFACE TO FIRST EDITION

Some twenty-two years have passed since the publication of *Medieval Figure Sculpture in England*, in which I had the honour of collaborating with the late Professor Edward S. Prior, and the book has been accepted as the standard work on the subject. It is now out of print, and in view of the growing interest in the subject as evidenced by the increasing provision for the study of art history in various universities, and above all by the Courtauld Institute associated with the University of London, there seems to be room for something in the nature of an abridged edition to serve as a text-book for students if such a volume can be produced at a price within the means of the modern purse.

The enterprise of the Cambridge University Press has enabled me to attempt to supply this need, and the fact that most of the blocks for the original work are available has made it practicable. Some 110 new photographs have been added, including several composite blocks from my paper on the Alabaster Tombs in the *Archaeological Journal* for 1923, in order to bring the story up to date and to add fresh interest. The plan has also had to be altered in order to bring the matter into smaller compass, so that it is really a new work rather than an abridgment, though still to a great extent based on the research, the results of which are set forth in the original book.

I must take this opportunity of paying a tribute to my late colleague, Professor Prior. It was a great privilege for me when quite a young man to have been associated with him in collecting and arranging the material for such a work. His wide knowledge and original mind were an inspiration and guide which I hope have kept me on a right course in these studies, and have certainly added a fascinating interest to my life.

A. G.

HARROW

January 1935

PREFACE TO SECOND EDITION

In presenting a second edition I have to thank many reviewers for their kindly criticism. It is gratifying that in very few cases have my conclusions or classification been questioned. One or two slips have been corrected, and I have to thank Mr J. G. Mann for helping me to bring some of the old-fashioned terms used in describing armour up to date. That the text of the book has been condensed, that descriptions which could be avoided by reference to the illustrations have been omitted, and that art theories and picturesque ideas which might have attracted the more sentimental reader have been rigidly excluded, are conditions forced upon me by the nature of the work and the necessity to compress into a handy text-book produced at a moderate price a subject with so many ramifications and covering so wide a field.

A. G.

CONTENTS

CHAPTER VI. THE LATE GOTHIC OR PERPENDICULAR
PERIOD

LIST OF ILLUSTRATIONS

ix

LIST OF ILLUSTRATIONS

xiii

LIST OF ILLUSTRATIONS

LIST OF ILLUSTRATIONS

Chapter I

INTRODUCTORY

(1) GENERAL REMARKS

Some American writers have treated English architecture as a mere provincial offshoot of that of France. Such an idea is both ill-informed and superficial. Even if we allow France a certain hegemony in art in the thirteenth century, our English work is no mere importation or copying of the French. No doubt there was frequent interchange of ideas and inspiration, but English church building took a line of its own which manifested our national characteristics and advanced by experiment on its own lines until it finally evolved the stately Perpendicular style, which has no counterpart on the other side of the Channel. All through we notice a strain of conservatism, a hesitation to carry principles to an extreme, and a loving attention to craftsmanship of detail, which differentiate an English cathedral with its wealth of mouldings and modest proportions from such a monument of overwhelming French ambition and logic as Beauvais Cathedral.

So, too, in the sculpture, while we can discern suggestions from abroad from time to time, the work on the whole follows its own course, fighting its own local battle against difficulties and overcoming them in its own way. Our sculptors seldom attained the complete mastery of technique which we admire in the splendid statues of Rheims, but sometimes the very struggle against technical difficulty, and the loving care bestowed on detail by primitive artists who are learning their art as they go along, are of more interest and charm than the more perfect productions of the experienced master.

We also have to face the difficulty that our English sculpture is in a much more fragmentary state than that of France, and we have to piece together our evidence of what it must have been like from broken and mutilated scraps or from the lesser carvings originally looked upon as of minor importance. In France much damage was done by Puritanic reformers, but it was not systematic, and many of the great porches have come down to us almost intact, apart from a certain amount of modern restoration, but in England all religious carving was deliberately and thoroughly destroyed under Acts of Parliament, and what we have owes its preservation to its inaccessibility or to its real or imagined secular intention. In one case, however, we are more fortunate than the French; the rage of the French revolutionaries was directed more against the aristocracy than the Church, and the tombs of the nobles were everywhere broken up and cast out, and usually have to be studied now in museums or in such collections of effigies and much restored fragments as may be found at S. Denis. In England the aristocracy never earned such violent unpopularity, and the tombs scattered all over the country, in parish church as well as cathedral, are a mine of wealth to the student of sculpture, costume and armour. They have suffered from neglect and careless mutilation, and more rarely from ill-judged restoration, but on the whole afford a very valuable guide to our subject in the absence of the religious sculpture.

The material for our study, therefore, consists mainly of the architectural sculptures and those of the monuments. We must not, however, forget that much of the sculpture most prized in the middle ages was to be found in the altar furniture and the decoration of the shrines of the saints, the productions of goldsmiths and metal-workers, or of the ivory and in humbler places the wood-carvers. This was especially the case in the earlier periods down to the middle of the twelfth century, for it was largely to the productions of what we may call the *cloister crafts*, made for and preserved in the monasteries, that the stone sculptors looked for their models when the growing ambition of the great church-building era led to the demand for larger and more effective sculptural decoration in stone. A few bronze tomb figures, some small ivory statuettes, a few broken wood figures and a number of late alabaster panels, helped out by some fine medieval seals, are all we have by which to judge of the vast riches which once decorated our cathedrals and abbeys, and it is tantalising to read of the gold and jewels removed from Becket's shrine at Canterbury by Henry VIII's commissioners, which filled twenty-six carts, or of

Fig. 1. Seal of Roger de Quinci, Earl of Winchester. 1219–1264.

Henry III's magnificent golden shrine of the Confessor at Westminster, surrounded by statues of gold and studded with precious stones.[1] The magnificent seal of the Earl of Winchester (Fig. 1) may serve to give some idea of the skill of the metal-worker of the middle of the thirteenth century, and a reference to the ivory carvings (Fig. 329) and the bronze or laton effigies (Figs. 320, 322, 399, 405) illustrated later on will also give some evidence as to the quality of the numerous priceless works of art which fell victims to the avarice of Henry VIII and the misguided zeal of the Puritan reformers.

[1] Descriptions exist of Bishop Stigand's great silver cross at Winchester in 1070, and in 1326 Bishop Stapledon set up a silver reredos.

Although this volume, for the sake of convenience, is devoted to the history of *sculpture*, we must beware of isolating it as the art of a specialist in the modern sense. Medieval art was a comprehensive whole with all its branches closely associated. In the greatest period sculpture was part of the mason's trade, and it was only as his technical skill increased that the *imager* became a specialist. Medieval sculpture should, therefore, be regarded as part and parcel of the building trade, just as in the darker ages which preceded the great twelfth and thirteenth century renaissance it had been mainly part of the craft of the gold- and silversmith, and architectural sculpture must not be too rigidly separated from its constructional surroundings if its full value is to be properly appreciated. The best figure work is mainly in building stone, not marble, and was usually intended to be finished in gesso and colour in order to be effective in its place in the building: it loses considerably, therefore, if transplanted to a museum and placed beside statues of marble meant to stand alone or finished with the delicacy of a Greek chisel.

It is, perhaps, something of a shock to those who have not studied medieval art to realise that all the sculpture, like that of the Greeks, was originally coloured. The fact that when the Classical marbles were first dug up the colour had faded led the connoisseurs of the Renaissance period to assume that statues should be left in the natural colour of the material. We must, however, realise that this was by no means the view in the middle ages. Modern attempts to restore the original colour have not always been successful, either through coarse craftsmanship, or a mere copying of what was left of the ground colour without the gilding and brilliant finish in bright pure colours of the original, and we shall best be able to gather an impression of the scheme adopted by turning to the illuminated manuscripts of the period. The recent cleaning of the interior of Westminster Abbey has brought out vivid traces of colour and gilded patterns on the tombs and other sculptures, and there can be little doubt that the exterior carvings of porch and façade were treated

in the same way. When Sir W. St John Hope and Prof. Lethaby[1]
examined the front of Wells Cathedral from a scaffolding they found
traces of a colour wash over the whole surface and signs of painting
and gilding over it. The whole façade must have resembled a colossal
reredos glowing with brilliant colours and a splendour we can hardly
imagine. The chapter-house doorway at Westminster is known to
have been painted and gilded, and in fact in our climate this protective
covering of the surface is almost necessary if the sculpture is to survive.
It is not uncommon to see a bit of modern restoration crumbling
away more quickly than the older work beside it, and this may be
due more to its never having had a protective wash than to any
lack of experience in selecting the stone. As soon as the masons had
completed their work the *whiteners* were put on, and they were followed by the painters and gilders.[2]

(2) THE SUBJECTS OF THE SCULPTURES

The study of the art of the past has other interest beside the purely
historical and aesthetic appeal. It usually casts light on the conditions
of life of the men who produced it, and, above all it enshrines their
ideals and embodies the thoughts and aspirations which occupied
their minds. The first thing to notice is the way in which the Church
dominated the whole life of the middle ages. In the absence of all
the distractions of modern work and play, without newspapers or
facilities for travel, with books scarce and difficult to read, men's
thoughts turned mainly to religious topics when not occupied with
war or the struggle for subsistence. It is mainly, therefore, in the
churches that we find the art of the day best exhibited, and the
subjects with which it deals are mainly religious or connected in
some way with ecclesiastic teaching.

[1] See Hope and Lethaby in *Archaeologia*, LIX, 1904.
[2] See Lethaby, *Westminster Abbey Re-examined*, chapters IV and XI.

Owing to the wholesale destruction of our more serious sculptures we have few such complete summaries of theological ideas as are found in the great porches of Chartres or Amiens, but at Wells, though the loss of attributes makes the identification of individual figures difficult, a few of the statues can be at least tentatively named and a general idea of the plan embodied in the great façade can be made out. The whole front of the cathedral is a vast theological scheme, worked out, no doubt, by Bishop Jocelin himself, grouped round the Coronation of the Virgin over the west door. The Apostles and Prophets who must have occupied the niches of the lower tiers are now missing, but the quatrefoils above them are occupied on the south side by scenes depicting the Old Testament from the Creation to the Flood, and on the north side by scenes from the New. Above them are two tiers of niches filled by large statues, among which Sir W. Hope and Prof. Lethaby [1] succeeded in identifying the Saxon martyr kings Oswald, Edward, Kenelm and Ethelbert, while St Eustace, St Thomas of Canterbury, and possibly St George can be picked out. As these are all on the north side and are grouped with a number of female saints, it is a probable suggestion that we have here the martyrs and virgins, while the bishops, monks and hermits on the south side represent the confessors. We find this same classification in the south porch at Chartres. At the base of the north tower the statues of the lowest tier have survived and comprise a group of grave bearded figures who might do for doctors of the Church, another of female statues, one of them carrying a pot of ointment, who are probably the holy women witnesses of the Resurrection, and a set of deacon saints probably representing St Stephen and his associates. Above the statues is a cornice of foliated niches all round the front containing reliefs of the General Resurrection—little naked figures rising from their tombs. The central gable has two tiers with figures of a somewhat later date representing the nine orders of angels, the twelve Apostles, and in the central niche at the top

[1] *Archaeologia*, LIX, 1904.

the broken figure of Christ in Majesty, the lord and master of them all.

Here, as elsewhere, the Bible scenes are mainly the story of the Fall, of how sin came into the world, and of the Redemption, concentrating on the Nativity and the Passion more than on the life story of our Lord, though there are one or two scenes at Wells dealing with the latter. A king and queen may, like the early statues at Rochester, be identified as Solomon and the Queen of Sheba, well-known types of the Old Law prefiguring the coming of the Magi to worship the new-born Christ under the New Dispensation.

At Exeter, in the fourteenth century, we have another great series of statues grouped round the Coronation of the Virgin, in which an absurd restoration has replaced the missing figure of Our Lady by a seated king. The upper tiers have a series of Prophets and Apostles, and the lower kings and warriors, who are probably Old Testament heroes placed here as ancestors of Christ, and not English kings as they have usually been called.

The bosses of the vault at Norwich illustrate the Old and New Testaments in a very numerous set of scenes, and the beautiful bosses of the cloister include a remarkable set of the Apocalypse. At Tewkesbury the nave bosses are devoted to the New Testament story, dealing with the Nativity and Passion scenes. These last are also common in the alabaster retables of our last period, where, if we restore the scattered panels of their proper sets, we shall find the Passion scenes, the Last Judgment, the Nativity forming part of a set devoted to the Virgin as the commonest subjects chosen, though others picturing favourite saints, and especially a series of martyrdoms, are fairly common also.

The last great collection of statues in Henry VII's Chapel at Westminster contains a new selection of saints with a number of interlopers added to the famous saints of the earlier period. These seem to have been chosen as having special powers of intercession in cases of plague or other troubles.

7

Even in the lesser carvings, where theological supervision was less strict, and more was left to the individual fancies of the mason-carvers, such as the bosses and gargoyles or misericord seats of the stalls, many of the subjects which appear at first to be merely legend and fancy had a theological or moral signification attached to them in the medieval mind. The strange monsters in the bestiaries were all given a somewhat far-fetched religious signification; thus the lion, who was supposed to bring to life his cubs, which had been born dead, by roaring over them, becomes a well-known symbol of the Resurrection, or the hunter pursuing the tiger and carrying off her cubs is said to distract the mother by strewing mirrors in the path, and thus becomes typical of the Devil who carries off our souls by setting before us the vanities of this world (see the misericord from Chester, Fig. 2).

There are a number of genre scenes, like the schoolmaster birching his boys (Fig. 3), but they are comparatively rare, and scenes from contemporary history are extremely unusual though they begin to appear by the fifteenth century. Thus we have the Coronation of

Fig. 2. Chester. Misericord. "The hunter and the tiger-cubs." *c.* 1380.

Fig. 3. Norwich. Misericord. "The Schoolmaster." *c.* 1420.

Henry V at Westminster on the chantry erected over his tomb, and the kings on the choir screens at Canterbury and York appear to be those of England since the Conquest and not those of Judah or Israel.

(3) THE SCULPTORS

Most art histories follow the lines laid down by such writers as Pliny and Pausanias in dealing with Classical art, or Vasari with that of the Renaissance in Italy, and allow the story to centre round the lives and personalities of a succession of famous artists. Their characters and styles, the influence they had on their pupils and the ascription to them of certain works, or an attempt to reconstruct others which have perished, form the main theme of such histories. But when we come to the medieval period this method will not work. Until quite the end of the middle ages no great individual artist seems to emerge head and shoulders above his contemporaries; we only know a few of the producers of the sculptures or paintings by name, and then only by accident where such names have been preserved as the recipients of payments in the royal or other accounts. We shall be dealing with the work of humble goldsmiths, masons, carpenters and shopkeepers, who were paid little more than their fellows who were

9

working on the plain walls and roofs of the buildings they were employed to adorn. As we proceed to deal with the successive periods we shall see that the functions of these various workers gradually change and develop, and researchers have dug out of the records and building accounts a certain amount of information which enables us to picture, at any rate vaguely, the conditions under which the medieval art we admire to-day came into being.

Down to the twelfth century the demand for art had chiefly come from the monasteries, and all through the dark ages the monasteries had been the main power to keep alive such technical and artistic traditions as survived the barbarian invasions and Moslem conquests. But the idea, once current, that the churches and all the works of art they contained were the work of monks can no longer be sustained. No doubt monasteries frequently maintained workshops and when the great revival came they were the chief patrons of the arts, but most of the work seems to have been done by lay workmen employed either as permanent servants or hired for the special occasion. It is true that in the early period monks are sometimes described as specially skilful in the arts, but this must probably be taken as indicating that it was an unusual accomplishment worthy of note. Where names are mentioned they are usually those of monks employed on what we may call the *cloister crafts*, such as metal work, ivory carving, book illumination, supplying shrines and altar furniture rather than the larger architectural sculpture. Great ecclesiastics like St Eligius and St Dunstan were famous metal-workers in their younger days, and in 1050 an abbot of Abingdon is recorded as "in auri et argenti fabrificio operator mirificus". In the thirteenth century Matthew Paris describes one Anketell, "monachus et aurifaber incomparabilis", as the maker of St Alban's shrine. One of the most famous of these monkish craftsmen was Walter of Colchester, a fellow-monk with Matthew Paris at St Albans. He started life as a goldsmith, but was brought to the abbey about 1200 to work at its treasures. He eventually became a monk, and was appointed sacrist in 1220, and finally became a brother in 1240. He is said to have worked with Elias de Dereham, afterwards Canon of Salisbury, on the superb shrine of St Thomas à Becket at Canterbury, completed in 1220.

Similarly in France we read of a monk "Guinamundus in architectura et sculptura peritissimus", and the shrine of St Lazare at Autun, of which three stone statues remain in a museum there, was signed by a monk by name Martinus, "lapidum mirabilis arte". On the other hand the finely sculptured porch at Carennac has a capital signed by "Girbertus Cementarius",[1] evidently a lay mason, employed on the church.

In England the fine twelfth-century font at Bridekirk is signed by one Richard, but he gives no description of himself (Fig. 4).[2] After the twelfth century signatures are almost unknown, and the best information about the sculptors has to be extracted from the royal accounts. Prof. Lethaby has given a most useful and detailed account of the masons and other artists employed on Westminster Abbey[3] in the middle of the thirteenth century. By this time there appears to have been a regularly organised lay trade in building. Henry of Westminster, the king's master-mason, Alexander the king's carpenter, and Fitz Odo, the clerk of the works, were in charge of a large body of men. In one week in the year 1253 wages were paid to 39 cutters of white stone, 15 marblers, 26 stone-layers, 32 carpenters, the famous painter John of St Albans, his partner with an assistant, 13 polishers of marble, 19 smiths, 14 glaziers, and 4 plumbers, besides 176 inferior workmen. Special jobs were often done by task-work, or as we should call it piece-work, and large sums were entrusted to those in charge of the works.

This seems to indicate that men specialised in their own particular

---

[1] See A. Gardner, *Medieval Sculpture in France*, Fig. 16.

[2] A bronze censer-cover found at Pershore, dating probably from the beginning of the eleventh century, is signed "*Godric me Wworht*".

[3] Lethaby, *Westminster Abbey and the King's Craftsmen*, and *Westminster Abbey Re-examined*. See also G. G. Scott, *Gleanings from Westminster Abbey*.

Fig. 4. Bridekirk (Cumberland). Font with the inscription of "Ricardus".
c. 1150.

job, and important figure work may have been frequently entrusted to specially skilled sculptors. Thus we read that in 1253 two images wrought by task-work cost 53*s*. 4*d*., and, as this date is that of the completion of the chapter-house, Prof. Prior suggested that these were the famous Annunciation group still extant (Figs. 197, 198). No name of the maker is given, and he is thus simply regarded as a skilled craftsman. The names which have survived are chiefly those of the clerks of the works, sometimes important ecclesiastics, and the master-masons, who were apparently men of some position. Though the latter had started life as ordinary masons, beginning perhaps in the quarries, they had risen by their skill and had evidently acquired a certain amount of education, so they were often made jointly responsible for the accounts, and were given special board and robes of office. As time went on they were often small contractors and evidently men of some substance, and in 1436 a contract between the Abbot of Bury St Edmunds and John Wode of Colchester, mason, provides that "the seyd John Wode schall haue hys bord in the Couentys halle for hym and hys man, for hymself as a gentilman and for his servaunt as for a yoman".[1]

There is, however, no evidence that the master-masons did the sculpture, though they may sometimes have had a hand in this as the most skilled part of the work. Makers of statues and tombs gradually began to specialise, just as the marblers of Corfe who provided the Purbeck marble were separated from the freestone masons, and as time went on they contracted for tombs or kept regular shops for the provision of sculptured wares.

The earliest names of London sculptors known to Prof. Lethaby were Thomas the image-worker and Richard his son in 1226. In 1257–8 John of St Albans, "sculptor of the king's images", received a robe of office along with Peter of Spain the painter, and Alexander the carpenter. Lethaby therefore assigns to him the credit of having

---

[1] *Archaeologia*, XXIII, 330–2. A careful study of the position and wages of the masons is to be found in *The Mediaeval Mason* by Douglas Knoop and G. P. Jones.

Fig. 5. Westminster Abbey. Transept. *c.* 1250.

carved the splendid angels of the Abbey transepts (Figs. 147, 148). He also suggests that in a fine bearded head there (Fig. 5) in a rounded cap we may have a contemporary portrait either of John of Gloucester the master-mason, or of John of St Albans the sculptor himself. John's masterpiece was no doubt the sculpture of the great north porch of the Abbey, of which we only have scanty records.

Half a century later we find the imagers separating themselves still more from the building masons, and we shall see the effect of this when we come to deal with their works in detail. Light is thrown on this period by the accounts of the Eleanor Trustees dealing with the erection of the famous crosses in 1292–4, which were published in *Archaeologia* as far back as 1842. Alexander of Abingdon, "le imaginator", was paid for the statues of the queen at Waltham (Fig. 237) and Charing Cross. It is possible that the statues of Charing

14

Cross were of metal, in which case he must have been a master of several crafts, for he was also paid for painting and iron-work. At Waltham he was associated with Dymenge de Leger "operarius". On the Northampton Cross, which still survives, the statues were made by William of Ireland (de Hibernia) "imaginator" and "caementarius" who was paid "pro quinque imaginibus ad crucem Northamptoni et alibi" (Fig. 238).

In the Abbey itself the beautiful bronze, or laton, effigy of Queen Eleanor was made by Master William Torel, goldsmith of London. He also made similar figures for Blackfriars and Lincoln, and received £113. 6s. 8d. for the three, a large sum in those days. He was also responsible for the bronze effigy of Henry III, placed on the inlaid marble tomb made by Peter of Rome. Of course it has been suggested by those who would belittle our English art that Torel was the Anglicised name of an Italian Torelli, but his family has been traced back for three generations of goldsmiths settled in London, and it should be clearly realised that at this date Italy had not yet produced artists capable of so fine a work.

In the fourteenth century we have records of the makers of the royal tombs. Queen Philippa's effigy was made by a famous foreign sculptor, Hawkin (or Hennequin) of Liège, who has sometimes been identified with Jean de Liège, one of the leading sculptors at the court of Charles V in Paris, where the individual masters of the Franco-Flemish school were beginning to receive more recognition than the old mason-craftsmen. Some little figures for this tomb were made by John Orchard, "latoner", or bronze-worker, and it is possible that he was responsible for the laton effigies of Edward III at Westminster and the Black Prince at Canterbury. He was also paid for the two small alabaster figures of the infant son and daughter of the queen, now in the Abbey, and this indicates that he was a versatile artist in varied materials unless he was head of an establishment which employed several workers and supplied tombs and other works of art to order. This was certainly the case later on, but at this period the contracts were usually made with a number of workers each of whom was to supply his own particular contribution. In 1395 Nicholas Broker and Godfrey Prest, citizens and coppersmiths of London, contracted to make the effigies of Richard II and Anne of Bohemia for the large sum of £400. The features of this were laid down in detail in accordance with the "patron" which they had shown to the king. The whole was to be richly engraved and enamelled, and little figures of saints and angels were to be provided. The marble work was to be provided by Henry Yevele and Stephen Lote, citizens and masons of London, for a sum of £250 besides a gratuity of £20 if it gave satisfaction.[1] These masons also received payment for the tomb of Archbishop Langham, whose effigy is of alabaster. Yevele was the king's chief mason, and superintended the building of the nave of the Abbey, and was perhaps the nearest approach to what we should now describe as an architect to be found in the middle ages.

For the fifteenth century we have the contract for the noble monument of Richard Beauchamp, the great Earl of Warwick, who died in 1439. Here again a number of different craftsmen undertake to carry out their several functions. John Essex, marbler, Thomas Stevyns, coppersmith, and William Austen, founder, covenant to make a plate of finest "latten" to lie under the image and a herse over it. William Austen also covenanted to cast and make an image of a man armed according to patterns, as well as the weepers about the tomb. John Bourde of Corfe was to supply the marble and bring it to Warwick and polish it. Bartholomew Lambspring, Dutchman, was to polish and gild the great image and the rest of the laton work.

We also have the contract for the Green monument at Lowick of 1418–19 (Fig. 6), between Katharine the widow with two clerks and Thomas Prentys and Robert Sutton, of Chellaston, "kervers". This is one of the fine alabaster tombs which are the chief feature of the sculpture of this period, and we thus see that it was provided by carvers working on the actual spot where the alabaster was

[1] Scott's *Gleanings from Westminster Abbey*, p. 174.

Fig. 6. Lowick, Northants. Alabaster monument of Ralph Green and Lady by Thomas Prentys and Robert Sutton of Chellaston. c. 1419.

quarried.[1] There was a regular trade in the fifteenth century in alabaster tombs and retables, and these were exported even to the Continent. Names of these "alablaster-men", as they were called, are known, and have been located in London, Norwich, York and other cities, but the chief centre of the trade was in Nottingham. As we shall see when we come to study their productions, the work was largely shop-work showing constant repetitions of types and technical mannerisms, but splendid in effect and sometimes attaining a high standard of workmanship, especially in the tombs.

More individuality, perhaps, was shown by the wood-carvers at this period, and the little figures on bench ends in the fifteenth-century parish churches or the misericords of the stalls of cathedral and collegiate churches display a spirit and invention which are rare in the larger sculptures. One or two of them have left us self-portraits. Thus at Great Doddington the carver is seated with the board across his knee on which he is working at a Tudor rose exactly like those on each side of him on the misericord (Fig. 7). Another example at Wellingborough, close by, is so like this that it must be by the same hand, and there is another carpenter at work with his tools about him at St Nicholas, Lynn.[2]

Finally, we find the citizen shopkeeper growing into a contractor, or business man working on a large scale. Thus Drawswerd, the imager of York, gave an estimate to Henry VIII for his father's tomb, which was never finished on the original lines. Now Drawswerd was mayor of York and a member of Parliament, and must therefore be regarded as the head of a considerable establishment, in which the actual carving was done by his shopmen and apprentices.

There is very little evidence of any elaborate guild organisation among masons and imagers during the medieval period. Master-masons seem sometimes to have had apprentices, and in the fifteenth

[1] A convenient abbreviated version of these contracts is given by F. H. Crossley, in his magnificently illustrated *English Church Monuments*. The original was preserved by Dugdale.
[2] Figured by F. Bond in *Woodcarvings in English Churches*, pt. I, "Misericords", p. 96. Now at South Kensington.

Fig. 7. Great Doddington. Misericord. Wood-carver.

century the masons had representatives on city councils, but the organised guild does not seem to have been really established before the sixteenth century.) In fact Messrs Knoop and Jones[1] describe the stone-building industry as having a capitalistic organisation from the outset, not easily reconciled with the democratic craft-guild system of the fourteenth or early fifteenth centuries.

This is not the place to deal with the problems of the medieval mason and the conditions under which he worked, as we are here dealing with only one phase of his activities, but this brief sketch of the development of the sculptor's position from the stone-mason striving to translate into stone the traditional subjects and types set him by his monastic employers, to the skilled mason or marbler of the thirteenth century, the specialised imager of the fourteenth, and finally to the shopkeeper or contractor of the fifteenth, is necessary to the full understanding of our subject. As we study the sculptures themselves we shall see these changing conditions reflected in the character of the art produced by each succeeding generation.)

[1] D. Knoop and G. P. Jones, *The Mediaeval Mason*, p. 159 and *passim*.

Chapter II

PRE-CONQUEST SCULPTURE

The period treated in this volume is from the earliest introduction of Christianity into these islands down to the Reformation—from the seventh to the first quarter of the sixteenth century. For the earlier part records are scarce and dating uncertain, but by comparing one thing with another we are able to make out a tolerably logical story of development. When we come to the post-Conquest period the steady advance of style makes classification easier and dating more certain.

Pre-Conquest sculpture in England may be roughly divided into three main categories, the Anglian cross-carving of Northumbria, the rougher crosses and more architectural sculpture of Mercia, and the later monastic style of Wessex. Fragments of carved crosses are found all over the northern counties and spreading into the northern midlands and the south of Scotland, and can be numbered by the hundred. The most conspicuous examples are the famous Bewcastle Cross standing in its original position on the moorland of Cumberland near the border, and the Ruthwell Cross in Dumfriesshire reconstructed from the original fragments in a little chapel near the spot where it had been thrown down by the Puritans in 1670. There has been considerable dispute as to the date of these monuments, as they stand entirely by themselves, unlike anything produced elsewhere in Western Europe at this early date. French critics until recently dubbed them as fine works of the twelfth century, while English critics have claimed them for the seventh. Recent research, however, has narrowed the possible dating to a period of about eighty years, from 670 to 750, which accords well with the history of the time.

The Northumbrian kingdom flourished from the middle of the seventh to the middle of the eighth century, and is made very real to us by the delightful picture presented in the writings of the Venerable Bede, who lived from 674 to 735. The Synod of Whitby, at which King Oswy rejected the Scottish rites, took place in 664, and Theodore of Tarsus (669 to 700) became primate of the united English Church. By the year 750 the Northumbrian kingdom was beginning to break up, and Mercia under Offa, 757 to 796, took the lead. In the ninth century the Viking incursions became more serious, and York was captured by the Danes in 867. Alfred (871 to 901) checked their advance and saved the southern and western parts from their ravages, but was compelled to hand over to them all the country north and east of a line drawn from London to Chester.

Alfred's successors gradually drove back the Danes, and Athelstan's victory at Brunanburgh in 937 and the recovery of York in 954 made England once more a single kingdom. Edgar's reign, 959 to 975, was a comparatively prosperous one, and was notable for the great monastic revival under the influence of St Dunstan, whose formidable figure dominates the scene until his death in 988. Fresh Danish incursions led to the supplanting of the old Wessex dynasty by Canute in 1017, but he was soon converted to Christianity and showed considerable zeal in restoring the churches he had burnt. He reigned as an English king and was succeeded by Ethelred's son Edward, known as the Confessor. He had strong Norman sympathies and was much under the thumb of the Church, and paved the way for the Norman Conquest of 1066.

Bearing these facts and dates in mind let us return to the sculptures and see how their development fits in with the course of history. It is now generally accepted that the best and most refined crosses date from the end of the seventh to the middle of the eighth century, corresponding to the bright interlude of Northumbrian civilisation so delightfully described by Bede. Rather less skilful work is then found in the Midlands under the Mercian supremacy, and in the latter part of the ninth century Danish influences affect the style. The later work in the north is poor and decadent, but in the south art schools arose in the monasteries reformed by Dunstan, which were in touch with Carolingian developments on the Continent. We will take these several schools in order.

SECTION I. THE ANGLIAN CROSSES

The Bewcastle Cross (Figs. 8, 9), to take the most striking of these monuments first, is a monolith shaft, some 14½ feet high, to which a cross-head was apparently attached, but is now missing. On the front are three sunk panels containing figures, in fairly bold relief, of Christ and the two St Johns, on the back is a vine scroll with birds and beasts pecking at the grapes, and on the sides are further delicately wrought vine scrolls and chequer and interlacing patterns. There is a runic inscription, so worn as to be hardly decipherable, but said to contain the names of several persons known to have been living about the year 670,[1] whence it has been suggested that the cross was erected to commemorate the conquest of Cumbria by the Northumbrian Christians. At Ruthwell the cross (Figs. 10, 11), which had been thrown down by the Puritans in 1670, has been re-erected, and a few missing parts restored, in a new church built round it. Here again are large figures of Christ in sunk panels on both back and front, in one case treading on the asp and basilisk and in the other with a clumsily wrought figure of Mary Magdalene wiping his feet with her hair. There are also smaller groups of two figures each representing the Annunciation, Visitation, and a scene of Eastern origin, St Paul and St Anthony meeting in the desert, very

[1] The usual reading makes it a monument to Alchfrith, son of Oswy, and the names of his wife and other contemporaries seem to confirm this interpretation. See note on p. 31.

Fig. 8. Bewcastle Cross, Cumberland.
c. 670.

Fig. 9. Bewcastle Cross. The "Christ".

rarely found in the West. There is a vine scroll with pecking birds very like that at Bewcastle. In both crosses the figures are quite well-proportioned and, if the execution looks a little coarse and heavy, this effect is partly due to the decay of the finer details caused by the storms and frosts of over 1200 winters. At Ruthwell there is a poem, the Dream of the Holy Rood, in runic letters, which must be one of the earliest specimens of the English language known, and also Latin inscriptions round the scenes. Prof. Lethaby has pointed out the similarity of certain letters in this last to forms found in MSS. of about the year 700.[1]

That work of such merit could have been produced in such a remote region, only recently converted to Christianity, comes as a shock to Continental students, but we need not take seriously the opinion of even so distinguished a critic as Rivoira who assigns them to the twelfth century. It is sufficient to point out that they do not stand by themselves,[2] but that there are many hundreds of fragments of more or less similar monuments scattered about the northern counties—there are said to be 500 in Yorkshire alone—and many of them already weather-worn and discarded were used as building material when churches were being re-built in the eleventh and twelfth centuries, as, for instance, at Kirkdale in Yorkshire where the church is dated by an inscription to the reign of Edward the Confessor, c. 1060. Now we have seen that the ninth century was one of turmoil and Danish invasions, so that we are thrown back to the end of the seventh and the eighth centuries as the one period of prosperity in which such numerous works of art could be produced. Bede, writing of the archbishopric of Theodore, says: "Nor were there ever happier times since the English came into Britain."[3] How then are we to account for this accomplished sculpture, for these vine

---

[1] *Burlington Magazine*, June 1912.
[2] The splendid cup found at Ormside, now in the York museum, must be dated to this period, and the MSS. like the Lindisfarne Gospels, which are more certainly dated *c.* 700, display a calligraphic skill in lineal ornament which has never been surpassed.
[3] *Ecclesiastical History*, bk. IV, ch. II.

Fig. 10. Ruthwell Cross. Fig. 11. Ruthwell Cross.

scrolls—for vines could hardly have been common in our bleak north-eastern counties at this remote date? It can only be accounted for as a foreign importation, and there are records of the importation of foreign craftsmen. Eddius tells us that Wilfrid introduced masons, and when in Rome in 680 "obtained from men especially expert a goodly store of sacred relics...and possessed himself after his wont of precious things too numerous to mention for the adornment of the house of God".[1] William of Malmesbury and Prior Richard of Hexham, writing in the twelfth century, state that Wilfrid brought masons from Rome, and Acca, his successor at Hexham, "enriched the church with manifold adornments and marvellous workmanship".[2] Benedict Biscop, when building the abbey of Wearmouth, of which the porch still survives, went over to Gaul and brought back masons to build a stone church "juxta morem Romanorum". He also sent for workers in glass, and went on journeys to Rome more than once to procure sundry fittings.[3]

Here then we have ample evidence of the importation of skilled workers from contemporary as well as later sources just at the period suggested by the Bewcastle inscriptions. The only puzzle then is that nowhere in Western Europe can any similar works be found dating from this period. Several observers have noted that the resemblance in style of these Anglian crosses is much closer to that of eastern than western models. We have already referred to the scene of SS. Paul and Anthony on the Ruthwell Cross, and the vine scrolls may be compared with those of Syrian mosaics, or such ivory works as the chair of Maximian at Ravenna, which is held to be a Syrian or Alexandrian production of the sixth century. There are also strong resemblances to Coptic ornaments, such as certain limestone reliefs of the fifth century in the Cairo Museum, where vine scrolls with

---

[1] Baldwin Brown, *Arts in Early England*, 1925, gives long extracts with translations from Eddius, set side by side with the later descriptions of Wilfrid's church at Hexham by the twelfth-century writers, Prior Richard of Hexham, Symeon of Durham and Aelred of Rievaulx.

[2] Bede, *Hist. Eccl.* v, 20. [3] Bede, *Historia Abbatum*, c. 5.

birds pecking at the grapes bear a remarkable likeness to those on the Northumbrian crosses. Mr Dalton in his *Byzantine Art and Archaeology*[1] also illustrates a wooden post with figures carved in panels dating from the fifth century in the same museum, which suggests the Anglian scheme. This eastern flavour is not so surprising when we consider the state of the world at the time. Gaul and Italy itself had been overrun by barbarian invasions and Rome was only a shadow of its former greatness kept alive by the moral authority of the popes. The seventh century was marked by the Mahommedan conquests of Syria, Egypt, Africa and Spain, which wiped out what had by then become the most civilised portion of the ancient world. Refugees no doubt had fled in great numbers into Italy and Gaul, and it is likely that when Wilfrid and Benedict Biscop came to search for craftsmen to build their churches exiles looking for work to support themselves would have been more disposed to follow them than natives of Gaul or Rome. Such men too would have been more skilled and therefore more welcome. There seem to have been Syrian colonies in southern Gaul, and in Rome itself at the end of the seventh and beginning of the eighth centuries four Syrians and three Greeks occupied the papal throne. Theodore, the first archbishop to exercise full authority over the whole English Church, after the defeat of the Scots at the Synod of Whitby, came from Tarsus, and his friend and right-hand man, the Abbot Hadrian, was an African and had presided over a monastery near Naples. These men reformed the northern Church in England, introduced Roman doctrines and music and no doubt also objects of art of the types with which they were familiar. Monastic institutions were of very high repute in the days of Bede and it must be remembered that the monastic idea first arose in the deserts of Egypt and the near East, where the hermits banded themselves together into groups for mutual protection.

The form of the monuments themselves seems to have been of

[1] Fig. 85, p. 148.

native origin. The idea of erecting tall crosses may have been Celtic, but there is no evidence of Irish sculpture which could have influenced the Northumbrian carvers. The Irish crosses are later in date and, like the Book of Kells which seems to have been derived from such works as the Lindisfarne Gospels, must have been inspired by the English monuments. As Mr Clapham remarks,[1] the Irish monks from Iona and Lindisfarne seem to have brought with them little but piety and learning, and it was only when the Greco-Italian element came into power after the Synod of Whitby that the great outburst of cross-carving took place. At Whithorn, the ancient Candida Casa, and at Kirkmadrine, in Galloway, there are some early crosses, some of which may go back to St Ninian's mission at the end of the fourth century, but their ornamentation consists merely of the sacred monogram with nothing which can be called sculpture. In the life of St Willibald, born about 700, it is stated that it was the custom of the Saxon race that "they are wont to have, not a church, but the standard of the Holy Cross, dedicated to our Lord and reverenced with great honour", and William of Malmesbury describes two crosses as standing in his day at Glastonbury, one of which bore the names of a seventh-century king and bishop. Preaching crosses, often probably of wood, seem to have been set up by the Columban monks, and we therefore appear to be justified in assuming that the great outburst of stone cross-carving of the seventh and eighth centuries resulted from the calling in of Wilfrid's and Biscop's eastern craftsmen to decorate the native type of monument. How far the surviving crosses were actually made by the foreign craftsmen, or how far by native pupils taught by them or working under their supervision, is a matter of conjecture. In the case of Bewcastle, Baldwin Brown thought the runic inscription pointed to native Anglian carvers, though the excellence of the figure-work might suggest

[1] A. W. Clapham, *English Romanesque Architecture before the Conquest*, p. 59. This book contains the best summary of our knowledge of the art of this period brought up to date.

the presence of a master doing some of the more important parts himself.

Under these circumstances it would be natural to expect the earliest crosses made by the foreigners or their pupils to be the finest, and that the quality of the work should deteriorate as time went on and the native carvers were farther removed from their teachers, especially as the Northumbrian kingdom began to decline by the middle of the eighth century. And this is exactly what we find. Prof. Brøndsted, the distinguished Danish antiquary, has made a careful survey and classification of the crosses in accordance with the development and decline of the foliage ornament, and especially the vine scrolls,[1] and his book enables us to arrange them in a more or less logical sequence. At the same time it would be wise to avoid falling into the temptation, so attractive to many continental critics, of expecting too logical a sequence of development or deterioration. The general position seems fairly clear within certain limits, but the classification of individual objects must be more or less tentative and conjectural.

A panel at Hexham (Fig. 12), with the lower part of what looks like a naked Cupid running among delicately twined vine tendrils, is probably part of the decoration of Wilfrid's church, wrought by his imported craftsmen. Brøndsted illustrates the Otley cross-shaft (Fig. 15) side by side with a very similar pattern from Maximian's ivory chair at Ravenna. There is considerable variety in the birds and beasts set in the vine scroll, and he is probably right in placing this cross in the first category, though the linear treatment of the drapery in the busts on the other side has not quite the modelling of that on the Bewcastle Christ. Side by side with this we may place the Easby cross-shaft, the various fragments of which are now safely

---

[1] J. Brøndsted, *Early English Ornament* (English translation). The most complete treatise on these crosses is W. G. Collingwood's *Northumbrian Crosses*. This is illustrated by hundreds of careful drawings by the author, which bring out the patterns more clearly than photographs of much weathered and decayed stones, though less reliable for detailed examination of the actual handling.

Fig. 12. Hexham (Northumberland).

collected in the Victoria and Albert Museum, South Kensington. Here the vine scrolls are exceptionally well wrought and the birds and beasts (Fig. 14) are full of life and vigour, while the grouped heads of the Apostles (Fig. 13) in spite of their worn condition suggest a level of attainment not reached again for 500 years. Brøndsted, accordingly, places this group at the end of the seventh century, and attributes them to the imported craftsmen, but he thinks that the scrolls at Bewcastle and Ruthwell (Figs. 8, 11) are a little coarser and should be placed in a second category early in the eighth century. It seems, however, unnecessary to separate them by more than ten, or even five years, which is a considerable period in the working life

Fig. 13. Easby.　　　　Fig. 14. Easby.

(Now at South Kensington)

of a man, especially as the work of a master and his pupil, even if contemporary, might show considerable variety in quality.[1] Without stronger evidence to the contrary, therefore, it does not seem necessary

---

[1] Baldwin Brown devotes the greater part of the fifth volume of his *Arts in Early England* to a minute and careful analysis of every detail of these crosses at Bewcastle and Ruthwell, with the collaboration of Prof. Blyth Webster in dealing with the runic inscriptions. He is satisfied that the latter part of the seventh century is historically the most likely period for their erection. He is also convinced that the reading of the runes to the effect that the Bewcastle Cross was set up in memory of Alcfrith, son of Oswy, may be accepted, especially as Alcfrith's wife's name Cyneburga also occurs. Alcfrith was under-king of Deira, and took a prominent part in organising the Synod of Whitby. He was a friend of Wilfrid, and is not heard of after 664, so that a date of 670–5 for the cross seems indicated.

31

Fig. 15. Otley.
c. 680.

Fig. 16. Jedburgh (Roxburgh).
c. 700.

to reject the evidence of the inscription which points to about 670 to 680 as the date of these famous crosses. A stone at Jedburgh, possibly forming the base of a cross, is a little coarser with birds pecking vigorously at the grapes (Fig. 16), and may be placed c. 700. Two crosses, one of which has a bird and vine scroll and the other a single vine scroll without animals, have been found at Abercorn, near Linlithgow, and as an Anglian see was established here for the short period 671–6, this seems the most likely date for the crosses.

Fig. 17. Durham. Acca's Cross. c. 740.   Fig. 18. York. St Mary's Museum.

The above is the most widely accepted theory, but it is fair to mention that W. G. Collingwood, whose lifelong study of the subject entitles his opinion to respect, places the whole series half a century later. He begins with a cross from Hexham, now at Durham, which has been identified with the one placed over Acca's grave on his death in 740 (Fig. 17). This has very refined vine scrolls, both single and double, but no figures or birds. A cross in private possession at the Spital, Hexham, is very like it, but has a much worn

Fig. 19. Rothbury (Northumberland).

Crucifixion on the back, and there are other fragments in the Durham Library from Hexham of similar style. Under this scheme the whole of the finest group of the Northumbrian crosses is brought into the second half of the eighth century, but this is not really necessary since, as Mr Clapham[1] points out, it is easy to suppose a second introduction of foreign craftsmen, especially as there is a record that Acca, who was Wilfrid's pupil, companion and successor, also did much to embellish the church at Hexham. The style is different from the bird and beast scrolls and looks like a separate inspiration.

Whatever theory we adopt there is little doubt about the subsequent course of events, even if there may be a little controversy about the exact dates. As the foreign school died out there was a

[1] A. W. Clapham, *English Romanesque Architecture before the Conquest*, p. 65.

progressive decline in the quality of the work. A cross at Rothbury of which we illustrate a portion now in the museum at Newcastle, shows a slight coarsening in treatment and a rendering of the drapery by parallel ridges (Fig. 19). A stone in the York museum (Fig. 18) has two huntsmen, one with a sword and the other girt with a horn,

Fig. 20. Ilkley.   Fig. 21. Aycliffe.

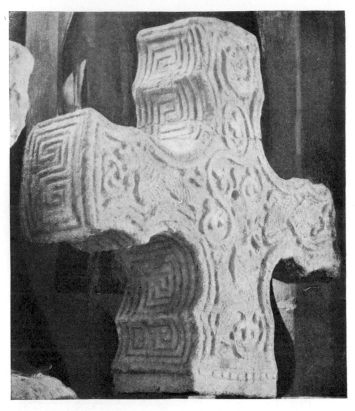

Fig. 22. Cropthorne (Worcs). Head of cross. *c.* 800 (?).

and a bold but rougher foliage scroll at the side. As time goes on
the scrolls become more and more formal, the beasts tend to become
less natural and their extremities melt off into meaningless interlacements. There is a tendency to divide up the face into panels, each
containing one, or sometimes a pair of beasts arranged almost
heraldically, as at Ilkley (Fig. 20). Norse inspiration begins to be
felt, and becomes stronger after the Danish conquests of the middle
of the ninth century. A cross-shaft at Collingham (Fig. 25) preserves

36

Fig. 24. Durham Library. Cross-head. *c.* 1000.

Fig. 23. Durham Library. Cross fragment from Gainford.

Fig. 25. Collingham.   Fig. 26. Eyam.

a reminiscence of the Anglian scroll, but mixes it with nondescript strap-like monsters derived from Norse wood-carving, and worked flatly in two planes, with rings marking the joints, characteristic of Danish work.

A cross-head preserved at Cropthorne (Worcestershire) of late Anglian type (Fig. 22) shows the shape of head adopted in all these early crosses, the wheel-head type familiar in tenth-century Irish crosses being mainly Celtic and later in date. The degradation to which sculpture fell as the Northumbrian kingdom dwindled away may be seen at Aycliffe, where the figures are little more than patterns (Fig. 21), or still more strikingly in a fragment from Gainford now in the Durham Library (Fig. 23).

A number of roughly carved crosses at Durham, of which we give one example (Fig. 24), must be mainly of the early eleventh century, as the see was only established there in 995.

Section II. The Mercian School

There are a few crosses scattered about the rest of England, but they are rare in the south. A fragment showing well-executed drapery at Reculver probably dates from the erection of the church at the end of the seventh century, but most of the others seem later and have little figure-sculpture.

In the northern midlands, however, there are a number remaining which there is reason to believe derive from the rise of Mercia to the leading position under Offa in the second half of the eighth century. The crosses at Eyam (Fig. 26) and Bakewell in Derbyshire may be cited as examples. In these the interlaced patterns continue, but the vine scroll has become little more than a bold spiral, while the figures are very rough and primitive.

Work of a purely Danish character may be found in the tall cross (Figs. 27, 28) at Gosforth on which episodes from Norse sagas are mixed with scenes of Christian origin. As good an example as can be found anywhere of early eleventh-century Danish style is in South-well Cathedral; it is a kind of tympanum now placed over a doorway in the north transept, and represents St Michael and the Dragon. The flat treatment and strap-like monster are very typical of a technique derived from wood-carving (Fig. 29).

A few examples of sculptured decoration other than that of cross carving have survived in the Midlands, some of which may go back to the second half of the eighth century or beginning of the ninth.

Fig. 27. Gosforth Cross. *c.* 900.   Fig. 28. Gosforth Cross. Detail.

Fig. 29. Southwell Minster. Over doorway inside north transept. *c.* 1000 (?).

The following century was too much taken up by the struggle with the Danes to have given much opportunity for church decoration. At Breedon-on-the-Hill some eighty feet of narrow carved friezes have been set in the walls of the later church. They have various interlacings and fretwork patterns, together with Anglian beasts and figures set in vine tendrils (Fig. 32). Most important of all are two larger reliefs, one of an angel and another a half figure, set under arches with bulbous capitals and raising their hands to bless in the Greek manner (Figs. 30, 31). This is a feature found in English MSS. of 750 to 850.[1] Some similar pieces, together with two figure-panels, are preserved at Fletton (Fig. 33). It has been suggested that they came from Peterborough, from the church destroyed by the Danes *c.* 870. Several pieces of a frieze of interlacements and animals are set in the south buttress of the chancel, and a row of busts reminiscent of those of the Easby Cross. The original situation for which these

[1] For full description of the Breedon sculptures see A. W. Clapham in *Archaeologia*, LXXVII, 1927. He gives strong reasons for dating them before the destruction of the churches of this district by the Danes in 874, and is inclined to favour the second half of the eighth century as most likely.

41

Figs. 31 and 32. Breedon.

Fig. 30. Breedon-on-the-Hill.

Fig. 33. Fletton.   Fig. 34. Fletton.

friezes were designed is not evident; possibly, like that at Hovingham,
which Brøndsted assigns to the earliest period owing to its Syrian
reminiscences, they formed a reredos. The panel figures have the
eyes hollowed to receive some kind of filling which is found in other

43

Fig. 35. Peterborough. The Monks' Stone.

Saxon work at Breedon, Wirksworth or Chichester (Fig. 34). The Monks' Stone at Peterborough (Fig. 35) is a shrine-shaped block with a row of figures under an arcade, derived ultimately from the design of a Roman sarcophagus.[1] The coped top is decorated with interlacing patterns which suggest a late eighth century date. Closely allied to this is a stone recently discovered at Castor, not far off (Fig. 36). The details of the arcade are very similar, but the attitudes are more vigorous and the drapery rendered by finer lines. The seated figure of Christ in a sunk panel at Barnack (Fig. 37) looks like an altarpiece, and may have been more influenced by Carolingian efforts in the south. This probably belongs to the post-Danish period of the latter part of the tenth century, to which the tower at Barnack may be assigned. Ruder and perhaps earlier work is to be seen in the remarkable slab at Wirksworth (Fig. 38). The subjects are diffi-

[1] A panel with two figures in curious head-dresses is also preserved in the cathedral at Peterborough, and evidently belongs to the same series.

44

Fig. 36. Castor. Fig. 37. Barnack.

cult to identify, but include the washing of the disciples' feet, a symbolical cross with the lamb affixed instead of the sacred figure and the four Evangelists with human bodies and beasts' heads, the Entombment, the Ascension, etc. This curious treatment of the Evangelists occurs also on a cross at Ilkley and probably at Edenham, and like the Greek blessing occurs in MSS. of 750 to 850.[1]

The coped tombstones with the figure of a bear at each end,

[1] Clapham, *English Romanesque Architecture before the Conquest*, p. 70.

Fig. 38. Wirksworth, slab.

Fig. 39. Reculver.   Fig. 40. Reculver.

known as hog-backs, of which good examples may be found at Durham, Gosforth and Brompton, appear to belong to the Danish period.

SECTION III. THE WESSEX SCULPTURE

There is very little in the south in the way of sculpture which can claim such remote antiquity as the crosses we have been discussing in Northumbria. The Reculver fragments (Figs. 39, 40) have been mentioned as almost certainly going back to the end of the seventh century, and are remarkable even in their mutilated condition as showing a high quality of workmanship. This cross stood inside the church in front of the apse, and the foundation on which it stood is contemporary with the pavement dating from about 670.[1] It was round in section, and the fragments preserved in the modern church at Hillborough show that it was not a monolith like the slab-crosses of the north. The figures in the scrolls are human, not birds and beasts, and the elaborate zigzag folds of the draperies, the careful rendering of the feet and variety of attitudes combine to give this cross exceptional distinction.

At Britford (Wiltshire) there are arches opening into porch-chapels with the jambs ornamented with a rough vine scroll, which may be dated to the beginning of the ninth century (Fig. 41). Crosses are scarce and the collection at Ramsbury have decadent ornament which cannot be very early. There is a tombstone at Whitchurch to a lady called Frithburga, with inscription, and a bust of Christ on one side, which might be early tenth century, but the most important remains seem to derive from the period of monastic reform under St Dunstan. Under his influence a brilliant school of MS. painting arose, in touch with the Carolingian schools on the Continent, and by the end of the tenth and beginning of the eleventh century the Winchester manuscripts had become famous all over Europe. Henceforth

---

[1] Fully described and illustrated by Sir Charles Peers in *Archaeologia*, LXXVII, 1927.

Fig. 41. Britford.

ornamentation is based more on a kind of semi-classical acanthus pattern, which takes the place of the Syrian vine scroll.

The little church at Bradford-on-Avon, now usually assigned to the tenth century, has two flying angels (Fig. 42) with napkins over their hands, a piece of Byzantine court ritual; these must have been placed on either side of a crucifix, or a sacred symbol, like the lamb bearing the banner. They resemble Byzantine ivories, and proportions are fairly natural. There is an angel in a very similar attitude built into

Fig. 42. Bradford-on-Avon. "Angel" over chancel-arch. *c.* 1000.

Fig. 43. Winterborne Steepleton.

Fig. 44. Langford (Oxon). Draped "Crucifixion". *c.* 1000.

the tower at Winterborne Steepleton (Dorset), which must have come from a similar group (Fig. 43), and at Deerhurst there is another angel in a fragmentary condition in a recess in the ruined apse,[1] showing that sculptured groups were beginning to come into favour as church ornaments.

The Rood, or crucifix flanked by Mary and John, without the flying angels, seems also to have been fairly common. At Langford (Oxon), a late Saxon church, there is one over the porch, and there is also a very remarkable Crucifix, now headless, draped in a long straight garment, with the hands very delicately rendered (Fig. 44). The well-known Romsey Rood (Fig. 45) is the finest of

[1] Illustrated by Baldwin Brown, *Arts in Early England*, 1925, Fig. 87.

50

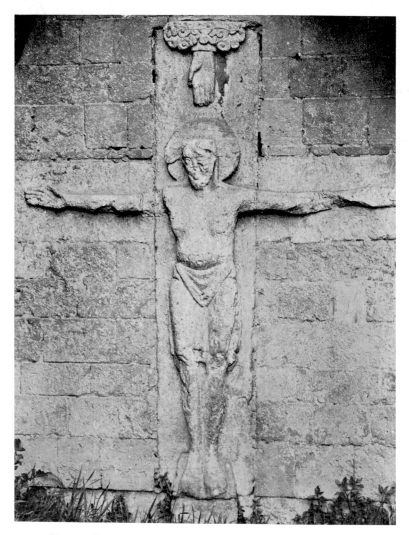

Fig. 45. Romsey (Hants). Stone "Rood" by side of south door.

these carvings; the proportions are correct and the whole a work of great dignity. It is far superior to anything produced in the half-century following the Conquest, and so seems to be rightly placed here, the only possible alternative being the end of the twelfth century. The feet are separate and not crossed, and the hand of God appearing from a cloud is an early feature, which is found in eleventh-century MSS. A stone slab at Stepney (Fig. 46) may be placed c. 1000 with more probability. When it is set beside such a Saxon ivory as the Deposition we illustrate from the Victoria and Albert Museum (Fig. 47) there can be little doubt as to a common inspiration if allowance is made for the different materials. The border is clearly an attempt to translate into stone the acanthus borders of the Winchester MSS.

A remarkable little relief in a smooth hard stone of the Madonna and Child at York (Fig. 48) is so unlike any of the rough Anglo-Norman sculpture that the pre-Conquest date seems probable. In spite of its mutilation it is a work of great delicacy, and the cushion and style of the drapery is more like late eleventh-century sculpture at Toulouse than anything else in this country.[1]

In St Nicholas' Church, Ipswich, several fragments of early sculpture are set in the wall of the present building. One is a tympanum carved with a wild boar, and another a panel with St Michael and the Dragon and an inscription in Anglo-Saxon describing the subject (Fig. 49). These show Danish influence in the spiral joints and other details, and are probably not earlier than the eleventh century.

We have left till last the most important examples of Saxon sculpture. Two slabs carved on built-up blocks of Caen stone, suggesting local execution, are set in the south aisle of the choir of Chichester Cathedral (Figs. 50, 51), and are supposed without any positive evidence to have come from the ancient Saxon cathedral at Selsea. They represent Christ coming to the house of Martha and Mary,

---

[1] Another Madonna at Inglesham and some rough figures of Christ and Apostles at Daglingworth (Glos) seem to be the work of rustic masons.

Fig. 47. Victoria and Albert Museum. Saxon ivory. The "Deposition". *c.* 1000 (?).

Fig. 46. Stepney Church. Stone slab. "Crucifixion."

Fig. 48. York Minster. Slab against east wall of choir.
2 feet high. "Madonna and Child."

and the Raising of Lazarus. In style they do not fit into any later
period, and certain early features seem to justify us in assigning them
to a date *c.* 1000, or soon after. One panel has a rough acanthus-

Fig. 49. Ipswich, St Nicholas. St Michael. *c.* 1000 (?).

Fig. 50. Chichester. "Christ coming to Mary's house." *c.* 1000–1050.

type cresting very like that on the rood at Stepney, and the way of emphasising the importance of the persons represented by grading them according to size points to an early date. The hair and other details are rendered with more care and variety than in Anglo-Norman work, and the high-shouldered attitudes and eyes hollowed out in order to be filled with crystals or jewels also occur in Saxon

56

Fig. 51. Chichester. The "Raising of Lazarus". *c.* 1000–1050.

sculpture elsewhere. The architecture of the house and capitals suggesting those of late Saxon date at Sompting, the zigzag folds of the draperies recalling those of the Winchester MSS. of *c.* 1000, the attempt to give expression to the faces, especially those of the weeping Martha and Mary, the use of the three-quarter profile, are all refinements which we shall not find again until we come to a period when art was so different that there could be no question of assigning these slabs to it. Moreover, the resemblance to such an object as the

57

Fig. 52. Victoria and Albert Museum.
Saxon ivory. c. 1000.

Fig. 53. Bishopstone, Sussex.
Memorial slab.

walrus ivory Adoration of the Magi at South Kensington (Fig. 52), work of some northern school, probably English, of the early eleventh century, provides another work of the same type, which we may reasonably assume to have had its origin in the monasteries reformed by St Dunstan, and in touch with the Carolingian schools of the Continent. A tomb slab at Bishopstone with doves pecking at a vase, a lamb and a cross, reminds us strongly of Byzantine motives and may, therefore, be placed here, though with less certainty (Fig. 53).

Fig. 54. Durham Castle. Capital in chapel. *c.* 1070.

Chapter III

THE NORMAN PERIOD

SECTION I. ANGLO-NORMAN SOURCES OF STYLE

The effect of the Norman Conquest on sculpture may easily be exaggerated. We must remember that the Normans were of the same stock as Saxons and Danes, though for a generation or two they had been in contact with Frankish civilisation. What we owed to the Normans was not the introduction of Continental refinement, but the impulse of vital energy backed by the spoils of the conquered race. This expressed itself in covering England with great churches on a scale hitherto undreamed of, but these at first were extremely plain and relied for their ornamentation on paintings or such barbarous, though effective, enrichments as the zigzag or billet patterns which are employed to decorate door-head, window or arch-mould. In Normandy itself there is even less early sculpture than in England, and when in course of time the stone-carver was called in to enrich the great buildings growing up on all sides he really had to begin afresh and look for new sources of inspiration instead of carrying on from such examples as the Chichester slabs. The first efforts of the Norman sculptor were of the crudest possible description, and such works as the capitals of the chapel in Durham Castle, *c.* 1070 (Fig. 54), are absurdly childish in comparison with the Saxon productions of the Winchester school.

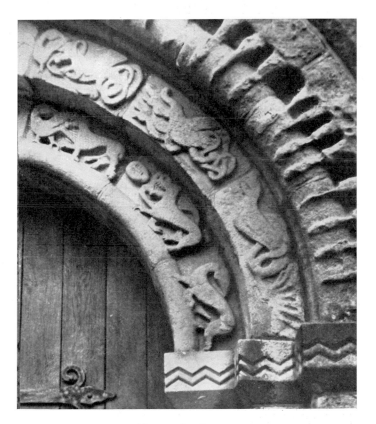

Fig. 55. Bradbourne.

In one indirect way, however, the Conquest introduced a lasting and decisive element into the history of English art; the Norman kings, in spite of their violence and excesses—perhaps partly because of them—were pious churchmen, and it was part of their policy to settle the country by founding monasteries to be centres of light and learning in the conquered territory. The eleventh century had witnessed a great expansion in the reputation and power of the Benedictine foundations, and especially of the reformed branch under the leadership of Cluny, and in the twelfth we see them at the height of their wealth and prosperity, housing themselves magnificently and showing themselves bountiful patrons of the arts. Their great churches, to a great extent, still serve as the basis of many of our cathedrals to-day, and it was their demand for architectural sculpture which stimulated the movement which developed into the Gothic building sculpture of the following century. Their influence, however, in this direction was not fully felt until the second quarter of the twelfth century, and may therefore be left to a separate section.

Although the first big abbeys and cathedrals were very plain we find a tendency in the smaller country churches to favour more elaborate doorways and fonts, and these, especially in the tympanum over the doorway, or in the mouldings round the door-head, seem to be inspired more by the old Norse carving of the later crosses than by Continental fashions. Such wild imaginations as the beasts with tails running off into interlacements, and carved practically in two planes, as we find at Bradbourne (Fig. 55), can only be derived from Norse wood-work technique, and even the more accomplished tympanum at Dinton (Fig. 56), with its beasts representing the souls of the righteous battening upon the "tree of life" and its St Michael fighting with the Dragon, or of Moreton Valence with its vigorous combat between a bearded long-robed St Michael and a dragon of true Danish type, carry on the old Viking tradition though amplified by the increasing technical skill of the carvers (Fig. 57). Mr Keyser

Fig. 56. Dinton (Bucks). Tympanum of south door. *c.* 1125.

noted over 240 of these tympanum carvings scattered all over the country, but most numerous in the western counties, and varying in style from quite accomplished work to the crudest village productions.[1] The reader must be referred to his book if he wishes to follow up this fascinating subject, as it is impossible to illustrate here more than two or three examples, such as the Entry into Jerusalem at

[1] C. E. Keyser, F.S.A., *Norman Tympana and Lintels,* 2nd edition, 1927, with 188 illustrations.

Fig. 57. Moreton Valence (Glos). Tympanum of north doorway.
"St Michael and Dragon." *c.* 1120.

Aston Eyres (Fig. 58) or the Samson and the Lion from Stretton
Sugwas (Fig. 59), which show the rapidly increasing story-telling
power that is such a feature of the later Norman carving. The beak-
head ornament, of which that at Iffley (Fig. 60) may be taken as
typical, also seems to derive from the bird and beast heads which
were such a favourite termination of Danish patterns in wood or
metal, as well as in stone or MS. drawing.

A remarkable group of these wild carvings is to be found in Herefordshire and neighbouring counties, and is of sufficient distinctiveness
to deserve special mention as a local school. It seems to be based
on metal-work designs with convoluted wire-drawn lines, while

Fig. 58. Aston Eyres. Entry into Jerusalem.

Fig. 59. Stretton Sugwas. Samson.

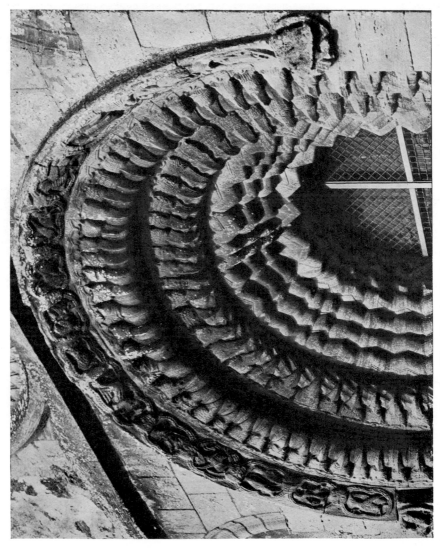

Fig. 60. Iffley (Oxon). Head of west doorway. *c.* 1160.

Fig. 61. Kilpeck (Herefordshire). Voussoir carving on south doorway.
"Zodiacal signs." *c.* 1140.

roughly-worked interlacing patterns of great boldness can be traced
back to Saxon or Norse prototypes.[1] The most conspicuous example
of this school is the little church at Kilpeck. Here the voussoir
carving on the doorway (Fig. 61), besides beak-heads, birds and
beasts, has the signs of the zodiac set in circles joined by grotesque
heads, which seem copied from a metal chain. The jambs of the same
doorway have shafts carved with a most astonishing collection of
writhing dragons and weirdly drawn-out human figures (Fig. 62)
set in foliage scrolls, which must have been inspired by such a piece

[1] Mr A. W. Clapham, however, in his *English Romanesque Architecture after the Conquest,*
pp. 141, 142, seems to regard this group as of purely Norman type.

5-2

Fig. 62. Kilpeck (Hereford). Jamb
of south doorway. *c.* 1140.

Fig. 63. Victoria and Albert Museum. Bronze
candlestick from Gloucester. *c.* 1150.

of monastic craftsmanship as the famous bronze candlestick from Gloucester, now in the Victoria and Albert Museum (Fig. 63). The shafts of the chancel arch are each composed of three figures of Apostles standing on one another's heads, in the same wire-drawn technique (Fig. 64).

The extraordinary fonts at Eardisley, Chaddesley Corbett and Castle Frome (Fig. 65), the latter standing on prostrate figures and carved with the Baptism of Christ and the signs of the Evangelists, are among the most effective productions of this school.[1]

In dealing with the Kilpeck carving it has been suggested that the sculptors were copying a metal-work model. This point is worth emphasising as it must be remembered that it was what have been called the cloister-crafts—works in metal, ivory, manuscripts, etc.— that kept alive the artistic tradition through the dark ages. Shrines, reliquaries, altar furniture, vestments and books were needed in the monasteries, and were brought away by monks flying before the Moslem conquests in Asia, Africa and Spain. When the twelfth century renaissance of art called for larger stone carvings to decorate the splendid new churches rising on all sides these smaller models were no doubt set before the masons to copy. Primitive art does not look to nature for models at first, but works in accordance with tradition, and we may therefore turn to such lesser arts for the origins of conventions which at first seem unaccountable and strange. Another excellent example of inspiration from goldsmith's work may be found in the richly carved capitals of St Peter's, Northampton, c. 1140 (Fig. 66).

It is a pity that the intrinsic value of the shrines and other products of the cloister-crafts in the precious metals have led to their being often melted down in times of stress, while the remainder fell victims

---

[1] Other notable examples may be found in the tympanum carvings at Rowlstone, Brinsop, Ruardean, Fownhope and Shobdon. It is on record that the Shobdon work was finished before 1148, which points to a date c. 1140 for this remarkable group. At Rowlstone there are also strange friezes of angels and birds.

Fig. 64. Kilpeck (Hereford). "St Peter" at side of chancel arch. c. 1140.

Fig. 65. Castle Frome. Font.

Fig. 66. Northampton. St Peter's Church. Capital of nave. *c.* 1140.

to the greed of Henry VIII. It is difficult therefore to set concrete examples side by side to demonstrate the point made above, but the few remaining objects in our museums, or the rather more numerous survivals in treasuries or museums abroad, enable us to form some idea of what they must have been like. We have already seen, when studying the later Saxon sculpture, how the drawing of the zigzag folds of the Chichester slabs (Figs. 50, 51) was influenced by the style of the drawings in the Winchester manuscripts, and such a monument as the Monks' Stone at Peterborough (Fig. 35) must be a stone copy of a metal shrine, while the birds drinking from a vase on the Bishop-stone slab (Fig. 53) repeat a motive of great antiquity, probably introduced by Eastern woven stuffs.

It has also been pointed out that the early Norman plain building relied to a great extent on painting for its decorative features. Traces of painting still survive on the extremely simple capitals of the transept at Ely, and it is almost certain that many of the plain cushion capitals of the period were decorated with painting, which would in some

71

Fig. 67. Westminster Abbey. Capital. The "Judgment
of Solomon". *c.* 1100.

cases have included figures. It was soon realised that such pictures
could be emphasised by outlining the figures by cutting back the
ground, or by strengthening the lines by incised grooves, and
we thus get such results as we see in the capitals at Westminster
illustrating the story of the Judgment of Solomon (Fig. 67), which
probably came from the original Norman cloister. Fragments preserved at Hereford suggest derivation from a similar source, as also
do the crude carvings on some of the capitals at Romsey (Fig. 68),[1]
and even the more advanced capitals of the crypt at Canterbury—
which are supposed by some authorities to have been carved in
position some time after erection, though this was not the usual
medieval practice—betray some signs of painter's technique. Here,
however, the stone-carver was beginning to feel his way to a style
of his own more suited to his material, and there are more attempts

[1] Other examples may be found on the capitals of the tower arches at Southwell,
Melbourne, Castor, etc.

Fig. 68. Romsey Abbey. Capital in aisle of choir.

Fig. 69. Canterbury Cathedral. Capital in crypt. "Samson."

Fig. 70. Canterbury. Capital in crypt.

at modelling in the round in the Samson (Fig. 69) and a feeling for composition which displays itself in the curious attempt to give symmetry by providing Samson with what looks like a floriated tail to balance that of the lion! The combat between the flying dragon and a dog on the other capital we illustrate is also a very vigorous composition (Fig. 70) and still retains some of the old Norse vitality in its new guise.

The painting technique of the capitals is also sometimes reflected on the fonts, and the shrine motive with figures under an arcade may be found at Hereford or at Burnham Deepdale, on the last of which each compartment is assigned to one of the agricultural labours of the successive months (Fig. 71). Fonts vary in quality from the crudest village workmanship like that at Hook Norton (Fig. 72), to quite accomplished productions like that at Burnham Deepdale or those to which we shall return in our second section at Coleshill (Fig. 91) or Southrop (Fig. 90).

A number of lead fonts form an interesting series: it is usual to

74

Fig. 71. Burnham Deepdale (Norfolk). Square font. *c.* 1100. "The Seasons."

find groups of them in which the same mould has been used,[1] though sometimes the figures and patterns are used in a different order. These may be illustrated from Dorchester (Oxon), where a number of seated figures resembling types found on twelfth-century seals are ranged under an arcade (Fig. 74), and from Wareham, where the font is hexagonal instead of round and the figures are in bolder relief and standing[2] (Fig. 75). Some of these seem to date from the

[1] F. Bond, *Fonts and Font Covers*, illustrated by 426 photographs and drawings, should be consulted by all those interested in this subject. Mr Bond noted 29 lead fonts, of which those at Frampton-on-Severn, Siston, Oxenhall, Tibenham, Lancaut and Sandhurst are all from the same mould. These are all in Gloucestershire. Warborough and Long Wittenham (Berks) are both from the same pattern. Ashover, Walton-on-the-Hill and Childrey are among the more interesting variations in type.

[2] Mr P. M. Johnston, F.S.A., thinks these were carved, not cast, and that this font may be an importation from France.

Fig. 72. Hook Norton. Font. Fig. 73. Brookland. Lead font.

middle or even the end of the twelfth century: one of the earliest examples would appear to be that at Brookland in the Romney Marsh, where there is a double arcade containing the signs of the zodiac above and the works of the months below (Fig. 73).

Mention must also be made of the fonts of black marble from Tournai in Belgium, though these were no doubt imported from abroad ready carved. There are seven of them[1] in this country, the most important being that in Winchester Cathedral with scenes from the legend of St Nicholas (Fig. 76). The style is firm but harsh, and as figure-work is not in advance of our native productions of the same date, *c.* 1150.

Corbel-tables, formed of a series of heads or grotesques, arranged beneath the eaves, are a feature of enriched Norman work. Good examples may be shown from Romsey and Kilpeck. In these the fancy of the sculptors has full scope and the old Norse imagination comes out again (Figs. 77, 78).

[1] Winchester, East Meon, St Mary Bourne, St Michael's Southampton (all in Hants), Lincoln, Thornton Curtis and Ipswich St Peter's.

Fig. 74. Dorchester (Oxon). Lead font. *c.* 1170.

Fig. 75. Wareham (Dorset). Lead font. *c.* 1170.

Fig. 76. Winchester Cathedral. Black marble font. *c.* 1150. "The Story of St Nicholas."

Fig. 77. Romsey Abbey (Hants). Corbel-table of choir. *c.* 1125.

Fig. 78. Kilpeck (Hereford). Corbel-table of apse. *c.* 1140.

Section II. The Later Romanesque

As we approach the middle of the twelfth century we find a more advanced type of work, influenced to some extent under cosmopolitan monastic inspiration by what was going on abroad, but at the same time retaining many of the old native characteristics. A gradual simplification of the elaborate conventions derived from the goldsmith and painter begins to show itself, though complete freedom is not reached until the following century. A more architectural feeling begins to appear in the sculpture, and the use of figure-work on a larger scale tends to become more frequent, and as it is produced by the building masons it fits naturally into the architectural scheme, and leads the way towards the great development of Gothic building-sculpture which was to follow.

We have seen figure-sculpture reaching considerable attainment on the capitals of the Canterbury crypt, and no doubt many of the monastic cloisters had a wealth of carved capitals. With the exception, however, of a few fragments like the Dark Entry at Canterbury, none of them has survived to compete with those of southern France or Spain, most having been destroyed at the Dissolution or replaced by later and more ambitious buildings. A few fragments survive to give us some notion of what they must have been like. We have already had occasion to refer to the primitive capitals from Westminster, and illustrate here one which came probably from Reading Abbey, now in the museum there (Fig. 79), which displays rather crude figure drawing with fine decorative effect, and another from Norwich, now preserved in the triforium of the cathedral (Fig. 80), which shows great delicacy of treatment and vigour of action, though the old linear handling of the drapery has not been altogether discarded.

One of the most ambitious efforts is to be found in the Prior's Door at Ely, leading into the cloister. It is surrounded by arabesques

Fig. 79. Reading.   Fig. 80. Norwich.

and foliage scrolls, with birds and beasts of the old Anglian cross tradition, but treated in a new way. The scrolls are no longer based on the vine pattern but on the acanthus, or still more on a trefoil leaf which afterwards developed into the Early English stiff-leaf foliage. Heads with staring eyes form brackets for the lintel, and the whole effect is rich and sumptuous. The tympanum (Fig. 81) has a beardless Christ in an aureole supported by angels, which still retains evidence of its manuscript origin. The lines of the drapery and little groups of tossed-up folds at the ends are still those of the Winchester drawings, and the extraordinary distortion of the angels' arms shows the inexperience of the sculptor in dealing with the problems of perspective when translating the drawing set before him into stone.

At the period we have now reached three main schools of building-sculpture may be distinguished, though the boundaries between them should not be too closely defined. They are the West-midland, the South-eastern and the North-eastern.

The *West-midland* is perhaps the most typically English in developing in its own way from the origins discussed above. The most impressive

Fig. 81. Ely Cathedral. Tympanum of Prior's Door.

monument is the great south porch at Malmesbury (Fig. 82). There seems to be no definite record of the date, but it must be in the neighbourhood of 1160-70. The outer door has no tympanum, and is surrounded by eight orders of mouldings carried right round the arch without a break for capitals or shafts. These mouldings are richly carved with foliage scrolls and interlacements, and three of them contain a large series of medallions with scenes from the Old and New Testaments. Here then for the first time we are confronted with a connected religious scheme evidently dictated by a learned ecclesiastic in accordance with the scholastic theology of the day in which events in the Old Testament were regarded as types or symbols

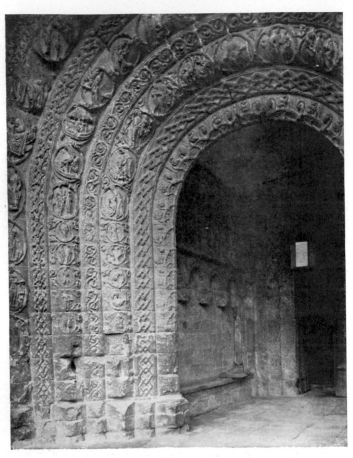

Fig. 82. Malmesbury Abbey. South porch. *c.* 1160.

of others under the new dispensation. Thus Samson carrying off the
gates of Gaza corresponds to Christ breaking through the gates of
the tomb (Fig. 83). This sculpture is weather-worn, and many of
the subjects difficult to make out, but the old cloister-craft technique is still in evidence. If we place such a figure as the Risen
Christ (Fig. 84) beside a contemporary manuscript drawing (Fig. 85)

82

Fig. 83. Malmesbury Abbey. The archway of south porch. *a*, Samson carrying gates of Gaza. *b*, Samson pulling down Temple (?). *c*, David rescuing lamb (?). *d*, David and Goliath. *e*, Entombment. *f*, Resurrection. *g*, Ascension. *h*, Pentecost.

6-2

we cannot fail to be struck by the similarity of treatment in the folds of the drapery, the double lines and smooth round patches over projecting portions of the anatomy like knees or thighs.

The inner door has a tympanum with Christ in Glory supported by two angels, but this is insignificant in comparison with the groups of Apostles ranged six on each side of the porch with a flying angel over their heads in the lunettes formed by the vaulting of the porch (Fig. 86). These are on a large scale, and some attempt is made to vary their attitudes as they turn to converse with one another, but the folds of the draperies are still partially rendered by incised lines, only the main masses being modelled over the figure and the pearled borders are a reminiscence of metal-technique. The bearded and closely-swathed angel is still rather clumsy, even as compared with his Saxon predecessor at Bradford-on-Avon, but in spite of a certain stiffness, and quaint details such as the way one of the Apostles has to bend his head to make room for the angel, the general effect of the group is quite impressive and there is a rough vigour in the design and execution which has more promise than the quieter elegance of the Saxon prototypes.

The next stage can be well seen in the doorways of the Lady Chapel at Glastonbury, built to replace the long-cherished wooden "Vetusta ecclesia", attributed to Joseph of Arimathea according to the legend, which was burnt in the disastrous fire of 1184. The new chapel was built in the most ornate late Romanesque style, in contrast to the choir begun at about the same time which is definitely in the Transitional style with pointed arches throughout. The north doorway[1] is very much of the same design as the Malmesbury door, except that shafts have been inserted in the jambs in two of the orders. The others are carried down to the ground and contain elaborate scrolls of foliage and figures, now too much broken to be clearly made out. The second order from the outside is slightly better preserved and shows a series of medallions enclosing scenes from the nativity cycle.

[1] Described by W. H. St John Hope in *Archaeologia*, LII, 1890.

Fig. 85. Illuminated figure-work from MS.
c. 1160.

Fig. 84. Malmesbury. South porch. "The Risen Christ."
c. 1160.

Fig. 86. Malmesbury. Spandrel-carvings at side of south porch. The "Apostles" of east side. *c.* 1160.

Fig.87. Glastonbury Abbey (Somerset). North doorway of Lady Chapel. "Herod." *c.* 1185.

Those of the Magi and Massacre of the Innocents (Fig. 87) show a definite advance in modelling and freedom of style, the metal-worker's technique and painter's tracings have been discarded, and we are well on the way to thirteenth-century style.

Some interesting reliefs are preserved in the Cluniac abbey of Much Wenlock from the lavatory in the centre of the cloister. One has two prophets or apostles under arches in the old shrine tradition, which are interesting to compare with a similar arrangement on the capitals of the great Cluniac abbey of Vézelay of half a century earlier date, though the actual handling is different (Fig. 89), and the other has Christ walking on the water (Fig. 88). The figures are short and heads too large, but they have just that mild suggestion of caricature which gives so much life and story-telling power to work of this date.

Monastic or ecclesiastic supervision is also to be seen in the subjects treated on some of the more elaborate fonts. At Southrop (Fig. 90), for instance, and on a very similar one at Stanton Fitzwarren, not far off, the Virtues are represented in human form trampling on or

87

Fig. 89. Wenlock Abbey. "Apostles." *c.* 1160.

Fig. 88. Wenlock Abbey (Salop). Lavatory cistern in cloister. "Christ walking on the water." *c.* 1160.

chastising the Vices, a subject taken from a poem, the *Psychomachia* of Prudentius, which was popular in the middle ages. Another font at Coleshill, near Birmingham (Fig. 91), is based on the design of the Gloucestershire lead fonts, but is interesting in having one of the figures in the cross-legged semi-dancing attitude fashionable in the southern French school of Toulouse and familiar to many pilgrims to the shrine of Santiago de Compostella in several of the statues in the famous porch built by Matteo in 1183. One side of the Coleshill font has a fairly advanced Crucifixion enclosed in a circle which still retains some reminiscence of goldsmith's work. Finally, in an

Fig. 90. Southrop (Glos). Font. "Virtues and Vices." *c.* 1160.

Fig. 92. Lullington. Figure over doorway.

Fig. 91. Coleshill. Font.

elaborate doorway at Lullington we see the figure of Christ removed from the tympanum and placed in a niche in the gable above; in this case the bas-relief has almost developed into the large statue of the next generation (Fig. 92).[1]

The *South-eastern* district of Kent was apparently more in touch with continental developments, though these influences are mixed and do not altogether efface the indigenous characteristics. The central monument of this group is the west front of Rochester Cathedral. The Norman church was consecrated in 1130, but the front shows signs of a reconstruction, probably after a fire in 1137. There was also a fire in 1177, but it is difficult to put any of the work as late as that. The capitals of the central doorway (Fig. 93) are decorated with foliage scrolls and animals of a type not unusual in rich Romanesque carving, but those of the archivolts are of a more peculiar type; in the inner ring especially there is a kind of ornament, half leaf and half bird, which is common not in Normandy or immediately across the Channel but in Poitou and Charente, notably on the façade of Nôtre-Dame-la-Grande at Poitiers.[2] We must remember that Henry I married his daughter Matilda to the Count of Anjou, and their son, Henry II, owned more territory in the west of what is now France than the King of France. It is not surprising therefore to find close relations between England and western France in the middle of the twelfth century. The tympanum has a Christ in Majesty supported by angels and surrounded by the Four Beasts (Fig. 94). This is in higher relief than we have hitherto seen, and in style the central figure is not unlike the seated statues in the arcades at Poitiers. In that region, however, tympanum carvings on a large scale are rare, and the general idea is more akin to those at Chartres or Le Mans, where we find the same scheme and the same lintel

[1] A rather more crude effort in this direction may be found in a slab-figure of a bishop in a niche over the north-transept door at Norwich; this must be earlier in date. It is illustrated by A. W. Clapham, *English Romanesque Architecture after the Conquest*, pl. 31.

[2] See the author's *Medieval Sculpture in France*, Fig. 131.

Fig. 93. Rochester Cathedral. West door. *c.* 1150–1160.

Fig. 94. Rochester Cathedral. Tympanum of west doorway.

with the little figures of the Apostles. We also have at Rochester statues of a king and queen (Fig. 95), probably Solomon and the Queen of Sheba, attached to shafts on the jambs of the doorway. This is a feature which became common in France and Spain after the middle of the century. The origin of the column figure is obscure; the earliest dated examples of S. Denis, if we may judge of them by drawings made before their destruction at the Revolution, were set up *c.* 1140, but look too far developed to have been the first experiments in the type. The Rochester queen has the same costume and long plaits of hair as the famous statues of Chartres and Le Mans, but the rendering of the lesser folds of the draperies by mere incised lines looks more primitive. As the knops of foliage on the shafts have

93

Fig. 95. Rochester. West doorway.
"Queen of Sheba."

Fig. 96. Barfreston (Kent). *c.* 1170.

been cut away to make room for these statues it is possible they were an afterthought added in emulation of the French works. If so they may be a little later than 1140, the date suggested by the fire, though they do not look as late as 1180, after the later fire.

A flatly treated statue, called Gundulf, is preserved in the cathedral, and seems to have come from a niche on the north turret. The drapery is very shallow in treatment, the richly ornamented vestments being incised rather than modelled, but it is interesting as one of the first of the great series of statues in niches which afterwards became one of the chief features of a cathedral façade.[1]

Rather later, in the third quarter of the century, we have the little church at Barfreston, which in general effect recalls the richly decorated churches of the Charente, south of Poitiers. The south doorway shows the international monastic type of decoration modified by what may be regarded as the English tradition. The tympanum has a seated figure of Christ in a vesica embowered in twining foliage in the loops of which are the heads of a king and queen, angels, and fanciful monsters (Fig. 97). The capitals with more monsters and tilting knights are effective (Fig. 98) and the medallions surrounded by foliage tendrils in the arch-moulds are occupied by quaint fancies and grotesque groups of animals playing musical instruments (Fig. 96) and so on, instead of the serious religious subjects of Malmesbury or Chartres. The keystone of the arch has a half figure of an archbishop, and inside the church is an amusing panel of a monkey and a donkey carrying a rabbit in a pail suspended on a stick (Fig. 99).

More serious sculpture is to be found on a white stone font at Brighton. It has a relief of the Last Supper (Fig. 100) of considerable attainment, and a Baptism and two scenes referring to St Nicholas on the other. The style cannot be matched by anything else in England, but bears some resemblance to that of the Tournai fonts, in which case it may have been a direct importation from Flanders.

[1] Another statue of about this date has been dug up at Sibertswold, near Canterbury. It is unfortunately in private possession and rather jealously guarded.

Fig. 97. Barfreston. South doorway. *c.* 1170.

Fig. 98. Barfreston. Detail of right jamb of south door. *c.* 1170.

The *North-eastern Sculpture* may best be studied at Durham, Lincoln and York.

At Durham there is very little figure-sculpture in the great cathedral, but the vault corbels from the chapter-house, infamously destroyed by the Dean in 1796, are preserved in a somewhat damaged condition in the library (Fig. 101). They take the form of "atlantes" supporting the weight on their shoulders, and their contorted attitudes would have been better appreciated looked up at from below than in their present position on the floor. A block with decayed figures about five feet high set back to back (Fig. 102) might have formed a corner post or shaft from a cloister, like those at S. Bertrand de Comminges in the Pyrenees. The most delicate work at Durham

Fig. 99. Barfreston. Carving in interior.

Fig. 100. Brighton. Font. *c.* 1170.

consists in some reliefs built up in the canons' houses and now removed to the library (Fig. 103). They represent the appearance of Christ in the garden after the Resurrection, and though there are still reminiscences of manuscript conventions in the folds of the garments and of goldsmith's technique in the beaded edges, the proportions and gestures are fairly correct, and the figures stand out from the background in true boldness of relief. It is suggested that these came from the original twelfth-century rood screen of the cathedral.

A delicately carved cross of late twelfth-century date at Kelloe (Fig. 104) forms an interesting contrast in style to the early crosses of this district, and is an obvious proof of the impossibility of accepting the arguments of the foreign critics who have assigned our seventh and eighth-century crosses to the twelfth century. The reliefs illustrate the story of the Invention of the Cross by St Helena.

The west front of Lincoln, like that at Rochester, is a composite monument of various dates. The severe eleventh-century façade of Remigius was reconstructed by Bishop Alexander, c. 1140–50, when the sumptuously carved western doors were inserted. Further alterations and additions took place in the thirteenth and fourteenth centuries. The most interesting feature is the series of reliefs forming a more or less continuous band over the doorways. These may not be in their original position as the order of the subjects is confused, Daniel in the Lions' Den being interpolated in the middle of the Scenes of the Flood, but they suggest that Bishop Alexander had planned an elaborate scheme of sculpture with bands in relief like those at Ripoll in Spain or Modena in Lombardy. Remains of a "Majesty" are preserved in the cloister, and may have formed part of such a scheme, as also, perhaps, a St John also preserved in the cloisters.

The long frieze, which is the chief interest to us, is composed of two series, one of which recounts the story of Genesis, and the other seems to be connected with the Last Judgment. The cloister fragments might have been part of a centre-piece to the last. The story

Fig. 101. Durham. Cathedral Library. *c.* 1150. Fig. 102. Durham.

Fig. 103. Durham. Cathedral Library. "Christ's Appearance
after Resurrection." *c.* 1170.

of Dives and Lazarus (Fig. 105) is in two panels; in one Dives
feasting with his two friends, and in the other devils pitchforking their
souls into the yawning mouth of Hell, while angels bear up Lazarus
to Heaven. There are also representations of the Descent of Christ
into Limbo, trampling Satan under foot, of Satan presiding over the
tortures of Hell, of the Apostles seated as assessors and of the Souls
of the Righteous in Abraham's bosom. The Old Testament scenes
include the Expulsion from Paradise (Fig. 106), the Building of the
Ark, Noah and family in the Ark (Fig. 108), God's Promise to Noah
(Fig. 107), Daniel in the Lions' Den (out of order interpolated among
the Flood Scenes), Noah cultivating the Vine, and inside the present
western transept on what was once the exterior of the Norman tower,
three men clinging to the trees up to their waists in the flood. The
style is bold and effective, and if the modes in the Expulsion scene
are a little stiff, the whole is full of vigour and expression. The

Fig. 105. Lincoln Cathedral. West front.
Dives and Lazarus.

Fig. 104. Kelloe (Durham). Cross.

Fig. 107. Lincoln Cathedral. "The Promise to Noah."

Fig. 106. Lincoln Cathedral. "Expulsion of Adam and Eve."

twelfth-century power of telling a story is here to the full, and the policeman-like gesture of the angel ordering Adam and Eve to move on, and the look of intense indignation on the face of Adam are altogether delightful.

Here again we see the connected scheme of medieval theology worked out in detail, in spite of missing portions, and notice how the power and learning of the churchman gradually ousted the semi-pagan motives of combats between good and evil symbolised by Samson and the lion, St Michael and the dragon and all the monstrous imaginations of the northern forests.

York has preserved little *in situ*, but the museum in the ruins of St Mary's Abbey contains some important pieces, and the remains of a great Doom subject have been unearthed in the Deanery and are now in the Cathedral Library. The latter consist of a shallow tympanum, considerably worn, with devils extracting the soul from the mouth of a corpse, and a large slab representing the tortures of Hell (Fig. 109). Gaping jaws at the side exhibit varied horrors, while inside a huge cauldron full of chained souls is resting on the flames which are stirred up by hideous demons at the bottom. At no other

Fig. 108. Lincoln Cathedral. Sculpture on west front. "Noah building the Ark", "Daniel in the Lions' Den", "The departure from the Ark", etc.

Fig. 109. York. Cathedral Library. "Doom" slab. *c.* 1180.

Fig. 110. York. St Mary's Museum. *c.* 1170.

period have the devils been so formidable as in the twelfth century, and these fearful imaginings help to explain the enormous power of the Church over the violent kings and nobles of the time.

A finely carved corbel in St Mary's Museum shows a struggle between a man and two dragons (Fig. 110)—the old symbolic combat, but treated with new power. The stone is deeply undercut, the subject is conceived in the round, not drawn on the flat, and we are now in the presence of a real stone-carver's technique.

More important still are a number of large statues of Apostles and Prophets found buried on the site of the south aisle of the abbey church. These may have come from a big doorway from the cloister to the church, or more likely to the chapter-house, and their date must be the end of the century. They include the few real column-statues existing in England, and show a great advance over the Rochester king and queen of half a century earlier. Heads are large and rather coarsely treated, hands and feet skilfully rendered and draperies well adjusted to the figure. The folds are boldly modelled,

106

Fig. 111. York. St Mary's Museum.
"Moses." *c.* 1200.

Fig. 112. York. St Mary's Museum.
"St John." *c.* 1200.

Fig. 113. York. St Mary's Museum. Fragment of "Virgin and Child". c. 1200.

with a tendency to rounded forms which might have developed from
those of such figures as the Promise to Noah at Lincoln (Fig. 107).
More than one hand could perhaps be distinguished as working on
them, the bold handling of the Moses (Fig. 111) and the St John
(Fig. 112) being rather different from the more refined and elaborated
treatment of one or two headless statues which appear to have been
set against the wall at the side of the doorway, but all must have been
contemporary. There are also the remains of a Virgin and Child
(Fig. 113) which may have formed part of a seated figure in the
central tympanum; the elaborate brooch and long plaits of hair
falling over the shoulders are those of Chartres, but the big-headed
broad prophets come from a very different school, and appear to
be a native development. Several voussoirs from the same door have
also been found, of which we show one depicting Herod giving

instructions to his soldiers for the Massacre of the Innocents (Fig. 114). Others appear to represent the Baptism of Our Lord and the Raising of Lazarus, and we have here, therefore, the débris of a great portal on the continental model, though it is difficult to trace foreign influence in the handling. It was, no doubt, easier to import general ideas than craftsmen to carry them out. This brings us to the threshold of the thirteenth century, which must be the theme of the following chapter.

Fig. 114. York. St Mary's Museum. Voussoir carving. "Herod." c. 1200.

Chapter IV

THE THIRTEENTH CENTURY (OR EARLY ENGLISH PERIOD)

Section I. Architectural Sculpture

The statues from St Mary's, York, brought us to the threshold of, if not actually into, the first years of the thirteenth century, and in them we recognise a vital change in the spirit of the work which henceforward is to be the characteristic feature of medieval sculpture. It is no longer applied decoration, such as it had been even when attached to the porches and doorways of the Romanesque period: it is now definitely architectural in character and definitely stone-carving, suited to the material of which it is composed, and no longer carrying on the conventions and tricks of the ancient goldsmiths' and painters' traditions. It was the work of the stone-masons engaged on the building, and seems to grow naturally out of the surrounding structure, marking points where emphasis is desired but not disguising structural features. It is this union of the sculpture with the architecture, this thorough understanding of material and suitability of purpose, which gives our thirteenth-century sculpture its unique charm. There is, too, an evenness of attainment which makes it difficult to separate local schools, though certain differences may be detected between east and west, but even these are mainly dependent upon the variety of materials available in the local quarries.

The storied capitals of the Romanesque period go out of favour in the thirteenth century. At the beginning we have at Wells a fine series of figures mixed with foliage, but the tendency was for foliage to be used more and more by itself for capitals, or even for simple moulded capitals to be substituted for more elaborate designs, though heads and beasts occur occasionally, and figures are used rather more

Fig. 115. Wells Cathedral. Capitals of piers in west nave. *c.* 1220.

Fig. 116. Wells Cathedral. Capitals in north transept. "Moses." *c.* 1220.

in corbels. The use of heads as stops for mouldings, or even as corbels, becomes a great feature, much more frequent than in France, though superb examples occur at Rheims.

Wells Cathedral provides us with some of the best examples of these features for the first half of the thirteenth century. The choir and eastern side of the transepts were begun *c.* 1185–90 and the work was gradually carried westward. The next section to be taken in hand was the west side of the transepts and the eastern part of the nave, down to and including the north porch, the date of which would seem to be about 1210 to 1220, though there may have been an interval during the Interdict from 1208 to 1213. The western bays of the nave followed soon after, and the whole church, including the west front, seems to have been completed in time for the consecration of 1239, though it is possible some of the more advanced statues of the front may not have been added before the middle of the century. Bishop Jocelin, in a charter of 1242, speaks of the work as finished, so that there cannot have been much left to add.[1]

The earliest work at the east end has been largely overlaid with fourteenth-century alterations, but the capitals are of the simple crocket type with little elaboration. Most of the figure-carving is in the capitals of the west side of the transepts and the earlier section of the nave. As the piers are of moderate height, these delightful carvings can be well seen, and have just that touch of caricature which gives such life and interest to the work. In some, fanciful heads or fighting dragons stand out among the foliage (Fig. 115), in others, serious Biblical subjects, such as the prophet Elias with head on hand and holding a scroll on which his name is inscribed, or Moses with the Tables of the Law (Fig. 116). The most famous of all are the man with a thorn in his foot—a subject which goes

---

[1] The chronology of Wells Cathedral has been carefully worked out by Dean Armytage Robinson and Dr John Bilson in the *Archaeological Journal*, LXXXV, 1930. It is possible that the Interdict in John's reign, 1208–1213, may be the explanation of the break in the style of the nave.

Fig. 117. Wells Cathedral. Capitals in south transept. *c.* 1220.

Fig. 118. Wells. South transept. *c.* 1220.

Fig. 119. Wells. Transept. *c.* 1200.

G

8

back to the days of ancient Greece—a man with the toothache[1] (Fig. 117), and a capital with thieves robbing a vineyard on one side and captured and punished by the owners on the other (Fig. 118).

Fig. 120. Wells Cathedral. East bays of nave. *c.* 1200.

Fig. 121. Wells. West nave. *c.* 1230.

The continuous triforium arcade has a series of heads forming the stops of the dripstone moulding, a somewhat illogical feature inside a building, characteristic of English as opposed to French work, but usually very effective. These heads offer a useful guide to the progress of the work and the increasing skill of the local school of masons, those at the east end of the nave being small and often retaining something of the archaic grin (Figs. 119, 120), while those to the westward are considerably larger and more accomplished works of art (Fig. 121).

[1] It has been suggested that these capitals had been damaged by the fall of the tower in 1248, and were re-carved *c.* 1280, because Bishop Bytton, who died in 1274, gained a reputation for curing the toothache, and this capital was re-cut to mark his tomb. The style, however, is entirely that of *c.* 1220, and it is more likely that the capital suggested the attribution of the miracle-working power to the tomb of the sainted bishop placed near it, than that the miracles suggested the capital.

Leaving the sculptures of the famous west front for separate treatment a little farther on, we must go back a little and trace the story of head, capital and corbel elsewhere. In the latter part of the

Fig. 122. Ely. Monks' Door. *c.* 1150.

Fig. 123. Oakham Hall. *c.* 1170.

twelfth century heads begin to emerge from the stage of the hideous masks of the Norman corbel-table, and such a head as that over the Monks' Door at Ely, or the severe heads in Oakham Hall (Figs. 122, 123) gives some promise of better things to come.

Heads from the eastern part of the nave at Salisbury (Figs. 124, 125), *c.* 1225, are almost contemporary with those at Wells, and here again slightly later examples from the clearstory at the west end show a rapid advance in skill (Fig. 126).

The introduction of Purbeck marble begins about this time to exercise a great influence on English work. A regular craft of marblers based on the quarries at Corfe, Dorset, and working both on the spot and in London and other big towns, exported shafts, capitals, tombs and other fittings to all parts of the country. In 1206 King John gave licence to the Bishop of Chichester to bring to his

8-2

Fig. 124. Salisbury. East nave. *c.* 1225.

Fig. 125. Salisbury. South-east transept. Freestone "head". *c.* 1225.

Fig. 126. Salisbury. West nave. *c.* 1240.

Fig. 127. Salisbury. Transept. Purbeck marble. *c.* 1225.

Fig. 128. Lincoln. Choir. Purbeck   Fig. 129. Boxgrove. Choir.
marble "head". *c.* 1200.   *c.* 1210.

cathedral "marmor suum per mare a Purbic". Elsewhere it is
spoken of as "marmor regis", and if, as seems likely, the quarries
were a royal possession, this may account for the rapid development
of the trade. The absence of good building stone in London, and the
ease of water carriage as compared with that over the bad roads of
medieval England, also helped its popularity. Under Henry III a
large body of marblers was working beside the free-stone masons
at Westminster, but the evidence of misfits at Chichester proves that
shafts and capitals were also imported ready made from the quarries.
The Purbeck marble is a dark shell limestone, not a crystalline marble,
but takes a polish, and probably first came into use as a native substitute for the dark marble of Tournai. The difficulty of working
a hard intractable material like this produced a bold firm style of
treatment, which set a good example for the free-stone cutters to
follow. The heads here illustrated from Salisbury and Lincoln (Figs.
127, 128) will serve to show the fine quality of this school, while the
strange harsh faces and conventional hair treatment from Boxgrove
(Fig. 129), *c.* 1210–20, and a rather later and more florid head from

117

Fig. 130. York. Archbishop de Gray's monument.
c. 1255.

Archbishop de Gray's monument at York (Fig. 130), *c.* 1255, may
show the influence of the marblers on their contemporaries working
in more tractable materials. The high quality of the free-stone heads
of the middle of the century may be seen in the examples given from
Lincoln (Figs. 131, 132) and Salisbury (Figs. 133, 134). A head in
the triforium at Westminster has already been referred to (p. 14) as
possibly a portrait of the master-mason of the day, or even of the
sculptor himself.

Corbels follow very much on the same lines as the heads. A late
twelfth-century Moses, with a long plaited beard and holding the
Tables of the Law, from Wimborne (Fig. 135), and a pair of angels
censing the head of Christ, from Lincoln (Fig. 136), *c.* 1230, show

118

Fig. 131. Lincoln Cathedral. Head in Angel Choir. *c.* 1270.

the enterprise and imagination of their authors, even if they are less architecturally satisfying than the more conventional angel patterns of the following centuries.

The spandrels of the wall arcades of our more sumptuous buildings also provided a useful field for relief sculpture, and deserve attention both for their technical qualities and for the subjects illustrated. The eastern transepts and choir of Worcester Cathedral were

119

Fig. 132. Lincoln. Angel Choir.
c. 1270.

reconstructed after the fall of the tower in 1175 and a fire in 1202, and were consecrated in 1218. The spandrels here, where they have escaped restoration, are of great interest as showing the first experiments of the thirteenth-century carvers in this class of work. In one

Fig. 133. Salisbury. Choir-screen.
c. 1260.

Fig. 134. Salisbury. Choir-screen.
c. 1260.

Fig. 135. Wimborne. "Moses."   Fig. 136. Lincoln. Corbel in transept. *c.* 1230.

Fig. 137. Worcester. East chapel. "Masons." *c.* 1210.

Fig. 138. Worcester. South-east transept. *c.* 1210.

scene a lady patroness (Fig. 137) is instructing a master-mason, indicated by his pair of compasses, and in the next one a monk is supervising the working mason, while in a third a bishop is presenting the model of his church at the altar. A very spirited series in the south-east transept depict the Last Judgment, with the Judge enthroned, the Last Trump, the Resurrection of the Dead, St Michael weighing souls, an angel joyfully escorting the redeemed to Heaven (Fig. 138), a devil escorting the damned chained together, apparently by his tail, to be cast into the mouth of Hell (Fig. 139), and devils roasting a condemned soul over a fierce fire. Draperies are rather tightly drawn and meagre and the whole treatment dry and angular, but the excited gestures and vigour of the attitudes show that none of the twelfth-century story-telling power had been lost, and the vigour shown in the Expulsion of Adam and Eve from Paradise

Fig. 139. Worcester. South-east transept. "The Mouth of Hell." c. 1210.

Fig. 140. Worcester. North-east transept. "The Visitation." c. 1210.

(Fig. 141) is unsurpassed. New Testament scenes, such as the Visitation (Fig. 140) and Presentation, in the north-east transept, are quieter and more restrained, though the affectionate greeting in the former is quite delightful. There are here some slight traces of the original colouring, and no doubt when this was new and fresh it disguised some of the harshness now apparent.

The wall arcades of the transepts at Westminster contained a number of these little reliefs of mid-century date, unfortunately much cut into and destroyed to make room for later monuments, and where they survive much decomposed by the London atmosphere. We illustrate one of the better preserved examples, showing a curious cramping of the little figures to get them into the triangular space (Fig. 142), as evidence that even at this date some sculptors were still in the experimental stage.

123

Fig. 141. Worcester Cathedral. South-east transept.
"The Expulsion." *c.* 1210.

Fig. 142. Westminster Abbey. Transept. Wall arcade. *c.* 1250.

The chapter-house at Salisbury has a series of the next period, *c.* 1270, but here the work has suffered severely from restoration. This was much more skilfully done than usual, and as the whole was painted and then the paint scraped off again, it is difficult to trace the genuine work without the description left by Burges of what he had accomplished when he undertook the restoration. The scenes illustrated here are selected from the more genuine pieces, and show that the balance and grouping are now very efficient and the whole full of liveliness and charm. The group of Lot and his daughters turning their backs on the pillar of salt (Fig. 143), in spite of Lot's new head, is a spirited version, and Pharaoh's Dream with the lean kine eating the fat ones and the thin ears of corn consuming the good ears (Fig. 144), and Noah's Ark which combines two parts of the story in one picture (Fig. 145), are fairly genuine, with the exception of Noah welcoming the dove.

Fig. 143. Salisbury. Chapter-house. "Lot." *c.* 1270.

Fig. 144. Salisbury. Chapter-house. "Pharaoh's Dream." *c.* 1270.

Fig. 145. Salisbury. Chapter-house. "Noah's Ark." *c.* 1270.

Fig. 146. Salisbury. Old choir-screen. c. 1260.

The difficulty met by the Westminster sculptor in fitting in his figures is really overcome in the most satisfactory manner by the use of a half figure of an angel, whose wings fill the narrow corners of a spandrel in a most effective way. The most charming examples of this scheme may be found in the old choir-screen at Salisbury, turned out by Wyatt but fortunately preserved in a side chapel. The sculpture is untouched and much of the original colour and gilding remains, and the coy expression of the angels (Fig. 146), the well-arranged draperies and fine heads below, combine with the knots of foliage and lovely capitals to make this screen one of the most perfect pieces of decorative architecture and sculpture that have come down to us.

Lincoln also had a fine series of angels in the elaborate wall arcades of the choir, but unfortunately they are badly mutilated or restored.

Angel sculpture reaches its climax in the great figures in the triforium spandrels of the Westminster transepts and of the Angel Choir at Lincoln. The former are the earlier and the finer, and may be dated 1250–5. Those of the north transept are slightly more severe (Fig. 147), those in the south more gracious (Fig. 148). In all the

127

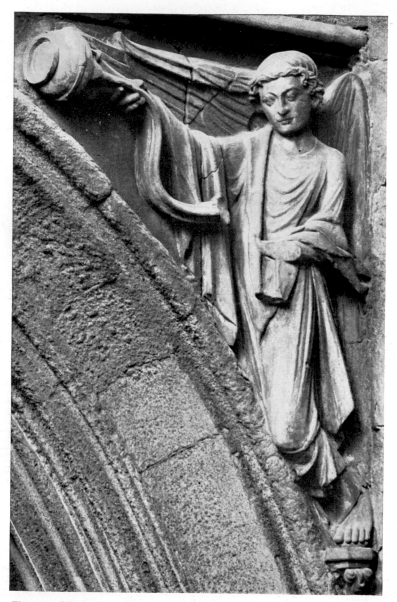

Fig. 147. Westminster Abbey. Triforium, north transept. "Angel." *c.* 1255.

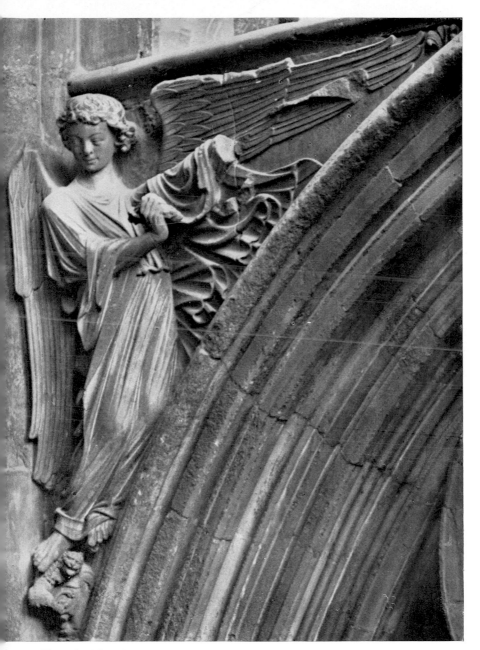

Fig. 148. Westminster Abbey. Triforium, south transept. "Angel." *c.* 1255.

Fig. 149. Westminster. Boss in Muniment Room. *c.* 1255.

composition, with swinging censer to occupy the corner and fluttering wings and draperies to fill the backgrounds, is masterly, while the firm treatment of the folds, and noble pose of the heads, make these angels the supreme masterpieces of English medieval art, fit to rank beside anything produced abroad. Like much thirteenth-century sculpture, they seem an incarnation of a new and noble type—the ideal which, as opposed to the sensuous, the trivial or merely pretty, may be called "monumental". They have something of the quality of Greek fifth-century art, when allowance is made for the difference in material and surroundings. They have recently been cleaned and considerable traces of the original colours and gilded star patterns have been revealed. Reference has already been made to Prof. Lethaby's suggestion (p. 14) that they may be attributed to John of St Albans, the king's imager at this period.

130

Fig. 150. Lincoln. Triforium of Angel Choir. "Angel of the Expulsion." c. 1270.

Fig. 151. Lincoln. "Angel of the Scales." *c.* 1270.

In the Muniment Room, adjoining the south transept, some exceptionally fine vault-bosses have recently been cleaned, revealing much of the original colour (Fig. 149). The quality of the work and style of the draperies prove them to have come from the same workshop as the angels. They represent lively combats with monsters and dragons. Vaulting-bosses are usually comparatively small and are mostly confined to foliage-carving until the latter part of the century. It will, therefore, be more convenient to defer further consideration of them until the next period, and return to the famous Angels of Lincoln.

Fig. 152. Lincoln. "Angel of the Resurrection." *c.* 1270.

The Angel Choir of Lincoln was begun in 1256 to accommodate the shrine of St Hugh and the pilgrims who flocked to it. It seems to have been completed by 1280, when the relics were translated to it in the presence of King Edward I, Queen Eleanor, and many of the leading personages of the realm. It is the most ornate building in any of our cathedrals.

There are five bays each containing one central and two half spandrels on each side. The work appears to have been begun at the east end with the bays which could be built outside St Hugh's apse, and then completed in a second campaign after the apse had been removed. The first idea seems to have been merely to house a series of heavenly musicians each playing a different instrument, but as the work proceeded westward a more solemn scheme was introduced and the objects held indicate the more serious activities

Fig. 154. Lincoln. "Angel and Christ."
c. 1270.

Fig. 153. Lincoln. "Angel and Madonna."
c. 1270.

Fig. 155. Lincoln. "Angel with hawk." *c.* 1270.

Fig. 156. Lincoln. "David." *c.* 1260.

of the angelic host. We thus have the angel of the Expulsion (Fig. 150), St Michael with the scales (Fig. 151), an angel holding up a little naked soul, probably St Hugh's (Fig. 152), and presenting it to the Madonna (Fig. 153), and another holding up the victors' crowns (Fig. 159). There is also a Christ showing his wounded side, to whom a little angel brings a soul (Fig. 154). But what are we to make of the splendid angel with hawk on wrist, which seems hardly in place in this august company (Fig. 155)? David, too, crowned and winged and holding a harp, finds his place in the heavenly choir (Fig. 156).

The angels were carved before erection in the usual manner, as is proved by certain misfits, especially in the wings (Fig. 155), and so were ready to be put in position when the building reached the

Fig. 158. Lincoln. "Angel." *c.* 1270.

Fig. 157. Lincoln. "Angel." *c.* 1260.

Fig. 159. Lincoln. "Angel of the Crowns." *c.* 1270.

required stage. The work of three or four different hands can be distinguished in them. Those at the east end who merely hold musical instruments or scrolls are evidently the earliest and are not very distinguished in character (Fig. 157). Figures and attitudes are sometimes clumsy and draperies soft and flabby as compared with the magnificent work at Westminster, though this is perhaps exaggerated in our photographs by the dust which had settled on them. There is a much more tense expression in the great angels of the western bays, and in spite of a little awkwardness in the perspective of the raised arms in the Expulsion and St Michael, which is less obvious when looked up at from below as intended, they are fine and forceful compositions. The flanking angel swinging a censer, which we illustrate

138

Fig. 160. Wells. West front. "Angel" quatrefoil. c. 1220–1240.

(Fig. 158), has a large head and is well composed, while the smaller heads and slighter figures in the Christ and Madonna seem to indicate the hand of another carver. Few traces of colour survive, but the stars on the background of the angel with the crowns (Fig. 159) show that the whole must have glowed with gilding and brilliant hues.

The idea of filling the spandrels with great angels came, no doubt, from Westminster, but the style is so different that they must be regarded as the product of a local school. The good stone available led to a rather more florid treatment in figure and foliage alike, which we shall notice again later in the north-eastern counties, while the firmer handling and sharp angular folds of Westminster may have been influenced to some extent by the bold and forceful technique of the Purbeck marblers.

Fig. 161. Wells. "Creation."

We must now return to our chief gallery of thirteenth-century sculpture on the west front of Wells Cathedral. We have already described the theological scheme embodied in it in our introductory chapter (see p. 6), but now have to examine it from a more technical point of view. Some critics brought up on the Ruskinian tradition are apt to complain that the doorways are much too small as compared with their French counterparts and that the whole design lacks the logical correspondence with the structure of the church behind of some continental examples. This, however, is not fair criticism, and ignores the idea which our English builders were trying to work out. Huge doorways are not suited to our northern

140

Fig. 162. Wells. "Noah."

climate, and what they were aiming at was a vast sculptured screen, like a reredos or altar-piece on an enormous scale. When fresh and new with the sculptures gleaming with gold and colours it must have produced an overwhelming effect, for, as already stated on p. 5, even outdoor sculpture was painted. When Sir William St John Hope and Prof. Lethaby[1] examined the front in 1904 they found traces of a colour wash over the whole which served as a base for the brighter colours, and incidentally helped to preserve the surface in our damp climate. The background of several of the niches still retained traces of having been painted red, and there were considerable remains of brilliant colouring on the sculptures of the west door and elsewhere. The placing of the western towers outside the aisles gives an impression of breadth and stability which is more satisfying in some ways than the narrower lofty façades of some foreign contemporary churches, and even the later completion of the towers fits in not unsatisfactorily. The bold buttresses break up the lines of the front and give the contrast and shadow which our French neighbours got from their cavernous portals.

[1] See their paper in *Archaeologia*, LIX, 1904, for a complete description from close observation from a scaffolding of all the statues, etc.

141

Fig. 163. Wells. The "Transfiguration".
c. 1220.

Fig. 164. Wells. "Preaching
of the Baptist."

The quatrefoils above the niches containing the lowest tier of statues are filled with half-figures of angels emerging from clouds and treated almost in the round (Fig. 160). They are of a strong masculine type, hold crowns or scrolls and are mostly clad in albs, the folds of which produce a rippled effect without any deep shadows—a method of treating drapery which may be taken as typical of the local Wells school.

Above the canopies of the lowest tier are large quatrefoils containing the groups of scenes from the Old Testament on the south side and from the New on the north. These are not real reliefs, but groups of

142

Fig. 165. Wells. Centre panel of north west tower. "Resurrection."

statuettes almost in the round except for the flat backs. They cannot, therefore, be compared closely with the spandrel reliefs of Worcester, but where sufficiently well preserved show more statuesque pose and dignity of composition. The Creation of Adam (Fig. 161) with its fine figure of the Creator and its suggestion in the heap of clay of the human form emerging from it is a masterpiece, and Noah building the Ark (Fig. 162), with his tools lying around him, is a delightful picture of a thirteenth-century carpenter at work. Among the New Testament groups the Transfiguration (Fig. 163) and the intent group of disciples listening to the preaching of the Baptist (Fig. 164) may be singled out for special praise. All the subjects are treated directly and simply with only the necessary accessories and no background beyond an occasional spray of foliage to fill a blank space.

At the top of the front is a cornice, supported by trefoil-headed niches enriched with beautiful foliage scrolls, and containing a representation of the General Resurrection, carried all round the façade. The little naked figures rising stiffly from their tombs display a lack of skill in treatment of the nude when seen from near at hand, which is not always equal to the rendering of the heads, but the general effect of the varied attitudes seen from far below is quite impressive (Fig. 165).

In the tympanum of the central door the Gothic quatrefoil has replaced the Romanesque vesica, and contains a Madonna, now headless, and on each side are censing angels (Fig. 166). Above the doorway is a broad niche, which looks like an afterthought as though it were felt that sufficient importance had not been given to the central feature. In this is a Coronation of the Virgin (Fig. 167), now headless, but showing the bolder treatment of drapery of the latest Wells school.

The statues are arranged in three tiers of niches, and 127 still remain, excluding the later figures of Apostles and angels in the gable. They are carved in the Doulting stone of which the Cathedral is built and must have been prepared either on the spot or at the Doulting quarries near Shepton Mallet. They are mostly about life-size, though some exceptionally tall ones are as much as eight feet high. These last may have been intended to correct the perspective when seen from below, or merely were made to fit the taller upper niches. In most such cases, however, a block, either plain or ornamented with foliage sprays, was inserted under their feet to bring them to the right position.

As we have noticed at Worcester and Lincoln there is a distinct advance in quality as the sculptors gained experience while the work was in process. The distinctive rippled Wells drapery is seen in process of evolution during the fifteen or twenty years from soon after 1220 to 1240 while the great work was in progress. The types are English and local, and though hints may have come from contemporary developments at Chartres or Amiens, the handling of details is quite distinct, and casual resemblances are to be accounted for by the fact that at the time thin draperies arranged in simple ways were in fashion, due partly to a reaction against the over-elaboration of the twelfth century. Although the work of more than a dozen different

Fig. 166. Wells. Tympanum of central doorway. *c.* 1220.

Fig. 167. Wells. West front. The "Coronation of the Virgin". *c.* 1240.

Fig. 168. Wells. Face of buttress.
"Noble."

Fig. 169. Wells. Face of buttress.
"King."

Fig. 170. Wells. South
panel. "Hermit."

Fig. 171. Wells. North
tower. "Lady."

Fig. 172. Wells. Head of Queen.   Fig. 173. Wells. Head of King.

hands can be picked out, there is a general similarity of treatment, which proclaims them all as the production of one workshop. Folds fall very straight with few deep depressions and often assume a V-form at the neck. Bishops are in mass vestments with the chasuble falling deeply in front, and ladies sometimes hold up a fold of their skirts, sometimes play with a necklace. Large, seated figures of popes and bishops, kings and nobles (Fig. 183) occupy the outer niches of the buttresses. Several of the kings have their arms akimbo in the attitude usually given to tyrants like Herod, but as Saxon saint-kings have been identified beside them we may merely describe this as a "Plantagenet" pose suitable for any royal personage at the time. The king we show (Fig. 169) is in a quieter attitude and is one of the finest of the series. The seated noble (Fig. 168) is also an imposing figure; as in most seated statues where the niche does not provide cover for too great projection of the knees the upper part of the body is some-

Fig. 174. Wells. Return of
buttress. "Bishop."

Fig. 175. Wells. Return of
buttress. "King."

Fig. 176. Wells. West return of north buttress.

what exaggerated in order to obtain the necessary perspective effect
from below. Several groups of four or more statues appear to have
been worked together like the four hermits (Fig. 170) on the south
side.

The earliest type of statue has large heads and flat faces, and may
be found chiefly among the bishops or abbots on the south side

Fig. 177. Wells. North
tower panel.

Fig. 178. Wells. East face,
north tower.

Fig. 179. Wells.
"Bishop."   "Lady."

Fig. 180. Wells.
"St Thomas of Canterbury."   "Warrior."

(Fig. 174), and in some of the standing kings (Fig. 175). Some very
tall ladies with small heads and rather stiff monotonous draperies
falling with little reference to the forms beneath, also appear among
the more primitive examples (Fig. 171). The head types may be seen
in Figs. 172 and 173. A more advanced series may be found in the
young nobles or princes grouped round the north tower (Figs. 176,
181), including the Saxon martyr kings. Some of the ladies, especially
those of the central panel, show more refinement (Fig. 177) and may
be placed beside some much more delicately modelled bishops with
smaller heads, such as the one beside one of the tall ladies (Fig. 179),

Fig. 181. Wells. Head of Noble.   Fig. 182. Wells. Head of Queen.

the fine figure on the central panel (Fig. 192), or the St Thomas of Canterbury (Fig. 180). Certain kings on the north tower (Fig. 178) and queens not far from them show more advanced character. The brows are more arched, the faces oval and eyelids carried straight across the bottom of the eyeball (Fig. 182).

On the whole the finest statues are those in the lowest tier preserved on the north tower. There are four grave, bearded personages who hold, or probably held, books (Figs. 184, 188) who would do for the Evangelists, or doctors, or, as one of a neighbouring group, which is more dilapidated, appears to wear a conical cap, we might label the whole lot as prophets. There are also four ladies, one of whom holds a pot of ointment and must therefore be Mary Magdalene (Fig. 185), the others probably being the holy women witnesses of the Resurrection. One of these has her dress arranged like the folds of the priestly chasuble; this device is used at Amiens and Rheims in the case of

153

Fig. 184. Wells. North-east angle-buttress.
"Evangelists."

Fig. 183. Wells. North-east angle of north tower.

Fig. 185. Wells. North tower.

Fig. 186. Wells. East buttresses of north tower. "Deacons."

the Virgin Mary, to give a kind of hieratic effect, and it is possible therefore that this Wells statue represents her. Finally there is a group of five deacons (Fig. 186), either the regular deacon saints

156

Fig. 187. Wells. Head of "Deacon".　　Fig. 188. Wells. Head of "Evangelist".

or the companions of St Stephen. These are interesting as displaying the characteristics of the Wells school in their fullest development. They are young men, tall and powerfully made, and the rippling of the Wells drapery has in them its clearest individuality. One has a slight moustache without a beard, which is very unusual in medieval art (Fig. 187).

The question naturally arises as to where this very individual school of Wells got its inspiration. We can see how, once it was started, development took place in the course of the work, but there is a great gap between such figures as the Malmesbury Apostles and the fully fledged statues of Wells.

There may be some reminiscences of metal-work in the fine lines of the draperies, and masons had had some practice on the capitals of the nave, but the immediate predecessors of the statues may be found in the monumental effigies, which by this time were beginning

157

Fig. 189. Wells. Recumbent effigy of "Bishop" in choir-aisle. *c.* 1200.

Fig. 190. Salisbury. Nave. Freestone effigy. "Longespée." *c.* 1240.

Fig. 191. Wells. North tower.
"Warrior."

Fig. 192. Wells. Centre panel.
"Bishop."

Fig. 193. Bristol. St James's Church. Freestone "Noble". *c.* 1240.

to be placed over the tombs of important people. At Westminster
we suggested that the bold lines and angular folds had come from
the Purbeck marblers, who were beginning to take the lead in effigy-
making. Now at Wells in the choir there is a set of bishop effigies
made not of marble, but of the local Doulting stone, and ornamented
with sprays of foliage which date them soon after 1200, when a set
to commemorate the first five bishops of the see was no doubt made
for the newly erected choir of the cathedral (Fig. 189). In these the
draperies are rendered by parallel rounded folds, not much different
from those of the Romanesque sculptures at Lincoln and York, but
the large heads and broad faces and general outline of the figures are
so like those of the earliest bishops of the front that these effigies would
hardly look out of place if set up on the front. Two other bishop effigies
were added to the series a few years later and in these there is some
advance towards the crisper rippled drapery characteristic of the
statues. A comparison, too, between the warrior in mail and surcoat
from Wells (Fig. 191) with the famous effigy of William Longsword,

160

Fig. 194. Winchester. Figure in feretory.

Fig. 195. Lanercost, Cumberland. "Mary Magdalene" in west gable. *c.* 1270.

Earl of Salisbury (Fig. 190), shows close affinity of style, while a civilian effigy in St James's Church, Bristol (Fig. 193), has exactly the same costume as the nobles of the Wells north tower. The tendency to tall proportions at Wells may therefore come from the effigies made to cover coffin lids or tombs, and it certainly looks as though the Wells statue-makers had learnt the rudiments of their art in the workshops of the effigy-makers either at Doulting or possibly at Bristol.

The story of West-country sculpture would have been carried on for us by the west front of Salisbury Cathedral, but the statues there have disappeared with the exception of two or three which are too mutilated for reproduction.

At Winchester a headless statue now in the feretory was dug up in the Dean's garden, and may serve to show a later development of the Wells style (Fig. 194). It evidently had a metal girdle, and possibly held a metal staff, holes for the attachment of which have been drilled in the stone. The freedom of pose and sweep of the drapery show an advance on the Wells ideal. Mr T. D. Atkinson has discovered that its base exactly fits a niche over the porch of the Prior's House, now the Deanery.

At Peterborough, at a great height over the three lofty arches of the front, a number of statues survive, which must be contemporary or a little earlier than the first school at Wells. They are of an entirely different type, and though drawn on broader lines for distant effect, they are evidently inspired by quite different models (Fig. 196). The broad flat folds, squat proportions and heavy nimbus behind the head can only have come from the wooden images provided for internal decoration.

We have already seen the high-water mark of our English sculpture in the angels of the Westminster transepts. This church combines the French plan with English execution in the details, and from the meagre evidence available this must have been the case in the great portals of the north transept, which was the main entrance to Henry III's new abbey, begun soon after 1245. Here there was a great triple portal on the lines of the porches of Amiens or Rheims, with sculptured tympana and life-size statues at the sides. There is a record that these included the Apostles, and it seems likely therefore that the central doorway followed the regular French scheme with

Fig. 196. Peterborough Cathedral. Statues on west
front. *c.* 1200.

a carving of the Last Judgment, while the side porches may have been
devoted to the Virgin and St Peter, the patron saint of the church.[1]
In the tympana, however, the French scheme of reliefs arranged in
horizontal tiers was not adopted, and Scott was no doubt correct
in reconstructing the modern doorway with the central figure in a
quatrefoil, but the lower part of the tympanum probably had a
number of smaller quatrefoils all containing figures. The mouldings
of the arch also probably contained little statuettes or animals embowered in foliage instead of in stiff niches placed one above another

[1] All the available evidence as to what this porch was like has been carefully sifted by
Prof. Lethaby in his *Westminster Abbey Re-examined*, ch. IV.

Fig. 197. Westminster. Chapter-house.
c. 1250.

in the French manner. Later French tympana, *c*. 1300, at Sens and St Urbain at Troyes have the sculpture arranged in tracery panels, but we can best form a notion of what the Westminster porch was like by turning to the south doorway of the Angel Choir at Lincoln, which seems to have been inspired by it.

Meantime, another doorway at Westminster leading from the cloister to the chapter-house has retained some of its original sculpture incorporated in the modern reconstruction. The tympanum towards the cloister had its ground covered with beautiful foliage scrolls on which were three brackets supporting a statue of the Madonna and two angels. One of the latter, minus head, remains in a very dilapidated condition. The inner doorway to the chapter-house is

164

Fig. 198. Westminster. Chapter-house. "Gabriel."
The Annunciation.

Fig. 199. Westminster. Chapter-house.
"Virgin."

mostly modern, but just above it are placed two fine statues forming an Annunciation, the dramatic discovery of which is described by Scott in *Gleanings from Westminster Abbey*, p. 41 (Figs. 198, 199). The wings of the angel are lost, but were probably of wood or metal; the groove for fixing them remains. The quiet immobility of the Wells attitudes and the soft clinging drapery have here given way to a bolder treatment and the sharp angular cutting which we have already seen in the other Westminster sculptures, and which we think was derived from contact with the Purbeck marblers, a specimen of whose work may be found in the heart memorial of Bishop Aymer at Winchester. In the chapter-house doorways twisted tendrils of foliage enclosing small figures of delicate workmanship fill mouldings round the arches or run up between the shafts on the jambs (Fig. 197). In one case they seem to represent a Tree of Jesse, but the arrangement is peculiarly English and more satisfactory than the superposed niches of the ordinary French scheme. It is tempting to trace the idea back through the foliage medallions of Malmesbury or Glastonbury to the primitive Saxon crosses.

The south doorway of the Angel Choir at Lincoln has been mentioned as probably inspired by the destroyed porch at Westminster. It is the only one remaining in England which can be classed at all with the French examples in scale, and even here it is a single door, not a triple portal. As already stated, this part of the cathedral was begun in 1256 and finished about 1280, and we shall be fairly safe in dating the sculptures of the portal 1270–80. The style is so different from that of the triforium angels with their smooth baggy folds that it seems likely that the sculptors of the Westminster porch came on to Lincoln when their work in the royal abbey was finished. Edward I was frequently at Lincoln in connection with his wars with Scotland and personally assisted in the translation of the relics of St Hugh to the new shrine in 1280, so that an importation of the royal masons to a work specially favoured by the king seems not unlikely. The tympanum (Fig. 200) represents the Last Judgment, with the Judge

Fig 200. Lincoln Cathedral. South doorway of Angel Choir. *c.* 1270–1280.

in a quatrefoil in the English manner, the general resurrection and angels conducting the souls of the blessed to Heaven on one side, and devils carrying off those of the lost, to be cast into the mouth of Hell at the bottom, on the other. New heads have unfortunately been given to the central figures, but in spite of this and the mutilation that the figures have suffered the draperies can be seen to be of the tense Westminster type, and the fluttering angels must have formed a very graceful and effective throng when fresh and gleaming with colour and gold.

Fig. 201. Lincoln. Judgment Porch.
"Foolish Virgins."

Fig. 202. Lincoln. Judgment
Porch.

Round the arch are three richly sculptured orders; the inner one has a series of queenly figures in niches more on the French plan, the next is composed of magnificently undercut foliage scrolls, and the third has beautiful little statuettes embowered in more undercut scrolls of the typically English thirteenth-century foliage. On one side these represent the Wise and Foolish Virgins of the parable, and on the other male figures difficult to interpret. These little figures have the grace and charm of Tanagra statuettes, and in their leafy housings form as delightful a series as anything the middle ages ever produced (Figs. 201, 202).

On either side of the porch are four magnificent statues, unfortunately headless and mutilated, but even in their present condition they demonstrate that their authors could produce something fit to stand beside the famous statues of Amiens and even of Rheims. They are placed on brackets, and are not column figures, like the French examples or those from St Mary's, York. Two of them represent the Christian Church and the Jewish Synagogue, typifying the Old and New Covenants. The Church (Fig. 203) stands upright with nobly flowing robes, holding a model of a church in her hand, and the Synagogue must originally have had bandaged eyes and held a broken staff and the Tables of the Law falling from her hand (Fig. 204). The contrast between the thick-fringed material of the outer cloak and the thinner garment falling about the feet is a new and splendid feature. The deeply cut folds and knotted girdle are found in a very similar, but more worn, figure at Crowland, which must have been almost a direct copy.

In the buttress niches to the east of the porch are three more statues from the same workshop, two of which have been restored as Edward I and Queen Eleanor,[1] and inside the cathedral a statue of an ecclesiastic in cope and alb (Fig. 206) must belong to the last

---

[1] The third is a lady in an unusual type of head-dress. At first glance one would suppose the head restored like the others, but this has recently been claimed as genuine. As the writer has not had an opportunity of examining this from near at hand, he must provisionally accept the verdict of those who have.

Fig. 203. Lincoln. South Porch of Angel Choir.
Statue of the "Church". *c.* 1270.

Fig. 204. Lincoln. Judgment Porch.
The "Synagogue". *c.* 1270.

Fig. 205. Lincoln. Judgment Porch. Statue
to east of entrance. _c._ 1270.

Fig. 206. Lincoln. Statue in chapel.
_c._ 1280.

Fig. 207. Salisbury. Chapter-house doorway. Sculpture of "Virtues and Vices" (Chastity and Truth). *c.* 1280.

quarter of the century. The restrained dignity of the treatment of the vestments and general pose belong to the great period of Gothic sculpture, but the realistic portraiture of the wrinkled face has more affinity to contemporary work in Germany than to that of the more idealistic French schools. The head carvings, of which our English masons were so prolific, must have given them a special skill in rendering faces and studying expression.

There is a fine mid-thirteenth-century statue in a niche in the west gable of Lanercost Priory, Cumberland, carved in the local red sandstone, but allowing for a rather coarser treatment necessary for its lofty situation somewhat reminiscent of the Lincoln style (Fig. 195). Prof. Prior has suggested that as Edward I was frequently in this neighbourhood during his Scottish expeditions and was at one time actually lodged at Lanercost, he possibly brought a sculptor with him from Lincoln to make what might have been a royal gift to the Priory.

In the chapter-house doorway at Salisbury there are a series of statuettes in niches round the door-head, set well back in a deep moulding. They represent the Virtues punishing the Vices, according to a poem by Prudentius called the *Psychomachia*, which was very popular in the middle ages. In our illustration Truth is pulling out the tongue of Falsehood, and Chastity is hanging Lust (Fig. 207). In spite of a certain amount of restoration these little figures retain much of their original charm.

SECTION II. THE PURBECK EFFIGIES

In dealing with head-stops (p. 115) we have referred to the work of the craftsmen in Purbeck marble as setting a model for their contemporaries, and we have again and again suggested their influence on the formation of the Westminster school of carving. Their most important production in the way of sculpture consisted in the recumbent effigies for tombs, which led the fashion throughout the thirteenth century for the greater part of England.[1]

Though early Christian churches grew up over the tombs or round the shrines of local saints or martyrs the custom of burial inside churches did not come into fashion until well on in the twelfth century. Abbots were generally buried in the chapter-house or cloister, but gradually the custom grew of placing the tomb of a founder near that of the saint or the altar, and very soon important persons left instructions in their wills for burial in a special church, in which, as time went on, chantry chapels were founded in which priests should continue to say mass for the souls of those buried within. In the great cathedrals which sprang up in the thirteenth century it became the fashion for a bishop to order a series of tombs for his predecessors, and thus we have already (p. 160) described a set made for Wells. There is another collection all of the same date at Hereford, and in France St Louis had a magnificent series of his ancestors made for the royal abbey of St Denis.

Among the earliest tomb covers is a slab of dark Belgian marble from Tournai, now in Southover Church, Lewes. It has an inscription with epitaph of Gundrada, Countess de Warenne, foundress of the Priory, who died in 1085. It has no figure work, but a decoration of acanthus-type foliage. This was apparently an importation, and it seems likely that it was obtained to honour a foundress some half-century or more after her actual death, and should be classed with the Tournai fonts which were described in chapter III. A slab at Ely with St Michael holding a soul (Fig. 208) in a dark-coloured stone may probably have a similar origin. It has a canopy over the head of the angel and is carved in a flat formalised technique, indicating a practised and established craft. The date is probably the middle of the twelfth century, or even a little later. At Salisbury,

---

[1] They were even sent abroad. The author has noted one in the north transept of Lisieux Cathedral in Normandy. Purbeck shafts also existed at Mont St Michel until replaced by restorers who did not realise what they were.

Fig. 208. Ely Cathedral. Memorial slab in south aisle of choir. "Angel holding soul." Blue marble—probably of Tournai sculpture. c. 1150.

Fig. 209. Salisbury nave. Black marble memorial slab. "Bishop Roger." c. 1140.

too, the effigy of Bishop Roger, d. 1140 (Fig. 209), is carved in the same formal flat way with foliage round the slab and a dragon at his feet. One hand is raised in blessing and the other holds a crozier, the butt end of which rests on the dragon's head. This must have been brought from Old Sarum to the new cathedral in the thirteenth century, when a new head in freestone seems to have been added.[1] Purbeck marble seems to have been introduced to replace these foreign importations,[2] and at Salisbury there is one of their early efforts in this line, probably the effigy of Bishop Jocelin, d. 1184[3] (Fig. 210). The style is ruder and more experimental, the lines of the vestments being simply incised, but the relief is higher, and it shows more promise than the sophisticated tradition of the Flemish workers. The effigy of Bishop Iscanus at Exeter, who died about the same time, is very flatly rendered, drawn rather than modelled (Fig. 211), and the face treatment of these early figures can be seen in the head of an abbot at Sherborne identified by an inscription as Abbot Clement, c. 1160 (Fig. 212).

The next stage may be seen in the tomb of Bishop Marshall (Fig. 213) at Exeter (d. 1206), brother of the Earl of Pembroke. This is in higher relief with the head projecting more above the slab, but the folds are still hardly modelled though represented more by ridges than incisions. Two little flat angel reliefs are placed on the canopy on each side of the head, and the tomb-chest is now richly carved with seated figures and heads in quatrefoils separated by sprays of boldly cut foliage.

Peterborough also possesses several of these marble slab-effigies over the tombs of abbots, c. 1200 (Fig. 214). In these there is some advance in the attempt to render the folds more naturally, the heads— some bearded, some clean-shaven—are bluffly and fully modelled, the

---

[1] The much worn effigy of Abbot Gilbert, d. 1121, in the Cloister at Westminster is also in black marble. See *Royal Commission on Ancient Monuments—Westminster*, pl. 202.

[2] It was known to the Romans, who used it in pavements. Fragments have been found as far afield as Verulamium (St Albans).

[3] Dates given under illustrations are only approximate. Tombs were often prepared during lifetime, and sometimes several years after death.

Fig. 210. Salisbury. Nave. Purbeck marble memorial slab. "Bishop Jocelin." *c.* 1180.

Fig. 211. Exeter. Lady Chapel. Purbeck marble memorial slab. "Bishop Iscanus." *c.* 1180.

Fig. 212. Sherborne. "Abbot Clement." *c.* 1165.

architectural canopies boldly carved, and the whole has something almost Egyptian in the strength and assurance of its conventions.

In all these effigies there is no attempt to give the effect of re-cumbency, and they would look more natural set up on end. There is, of course, no attempt at portraiture; in fact all through the middle ages types rather than individual characterisation are the aim.

Effigies of the second quarter of the thirteenth century may be found at Worcester (Fig. 215), Carlisle, Sherborne and Ely. These show a tendency to more elaborate, more natural draperies, and less of the Egyptian severity. There is also a decoration of the slab with more undercut foliage, and in the later examples, as at Sherborne (Fig. 218), there are some concessions to the recumbent position, such as the placing of a cushion under the head or allowing some of

178

Fig. 213. Exeter. Purbeck marble tomb of Bishop Marshall. *c.* 1210.

Fig. 214. Peterborough. Purbeck marble "Abbot". *c.* 1200.

Fig. 215. Worcester. Lady Chapel. Purbeck marble "Bishop". *c.* 1240.

Fig. 216. Ely. Presbytery. Purbeck marble effigy of Bishop Northwold. c. 1255.

Fig. 217. Ely. Presbytery. Purbeck marble effigy of Bishop Kilkenny. c. 1256.

Fig. 218. Sherborne. Purbeck marble effigy of "Abbot". *c.* 1245.

the folds to fall down on to the slab. The most gorgeous of all these Purbeck bishops is Bishop Northwold of Ely, d. 1254 (Fig. 216). Here the effigy is set in a kind of cradle of rich carving. The shafts of the canopy are foliated all the way down, and little figures in niches occupy the sides. Bishop Kilkenny, d. 1256, also at Ely, is a taller and slighter figure (Fig. 217) and has bold crockets of stiff-leaf foliage at the sides, but the finest of these mid-century ecclesiastics is Archbishop de Gray, d. 1255, at York (Fig. 219), who lies under a magnificent canopy in the south transept of the cathedral. This is difficult to photograph without distortion under the canopy, but our illustration shows that the standing posture is still maintained and that the figure, in spite of its masterly execution in other ways, is still a statue in a niche laid on its back.

The later phases of the Purbeck bishop may be illustrated by the tombs of Bishop de la Wyle, d. 1271, at Salisbury (Fig. 220), and Bishop Inglethorpe, d. 1290, at Rochester (Fig. 221). The former exhibits the smoother thinner draperies and overlapping folds then coming into fashion, and in the latter there is great simplification of handling, but the broad smooth surfaces of the drapery were intentionally prepared in this way to allow for surface decoration in

182

Fig. 219. York. Transept. Archbishop de Gray. *c.* 1255.

Fig. 220. Salisbury. Nave. Purbeck marble effigy of Bishop de la Wyle. *c.* 1270.

Fig. 221. Rochester. Purbeck marble effigy of Bishop Inglethorpe. *c.* 1290.

gold and colour. It was probably this tendency to gild and colour the surface which caused the end of the Purbeck marble trade. Beginning with gilded ornaments the addition of other colours tended to encroach more and more upon the surface until it was found that more easily worked freestone with detailed ornament worked up in gesso, or plaster, and coloured all over provided just as effective and sumptuous a monument as the more expensive marble figure.

Besides ecclesiastics, the Purbeck marblers produced knights and ladies. How far they were worked on the spot and how far in London or other big towns is not known, but probably both methods were employed. It is, however, purely a matter of conjecture if we try to assign to one or another district. Masses of chips and fragments have been found in digging foundations in the village of Corfe, which proves that at any rate much carving was done on the spot. The writer has notes of about eighty Purbeck effigies scattered over the country, without counting copies in Frosterley marble or other local varieties.

The earliest knights can best be studied in the Temple Church, London. These were cleverly restored by Richardson in 1842, but he has left us a description of the state in which he found them. The earliest one was in low relief with no cushion under the head and straight legs. The figure is covered with mail, with mail coif over the head and a surcoat of linen, or some such material, which was introduced during the Crusading period to keep off the heat of the sun.[1] This effigy was much decayed and is heavily restored.

The next in date, conjecturally assigned to William Marshall, Earl of Pembroke, d. 1219 (Fig. 222), is more genuine, though it was broken into four pieces and needed much patching. It shows considerable progress, but the pictorial representation of a standing figure is still retained. The legs are straight and there is some bold foliage on the slab, while a flat cushion is placed under the head, as the first slight concession to the recumbent pose.

[1] Another explanation is that it was required for heraldic devices.

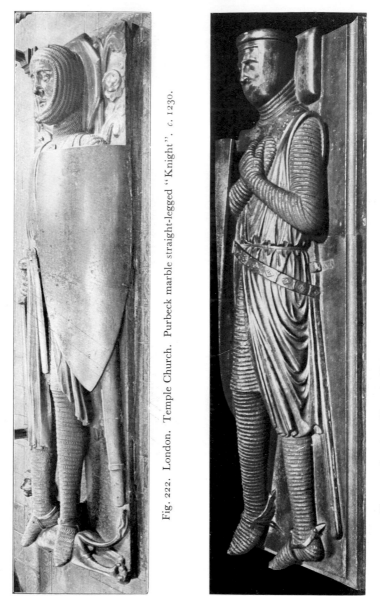

Fig. 222. London. Temple Church. Purbeck marble straight-legged "Knight". c. 1230.

Fig. 223. London. Temple Church. Purbeck marble cross-legged "Knight". c. 1245.

Fig. 224. London. Temple Church. Purbeck marble reclining "Knight". c. 1245.

Fig. 225. Sandwich. Chapel of St Bartholomew's Hospital. Purbeck marble "Knight". c. 1240.

Fig. 226. Walkerne (Herts). Purbeck marble cross-legged "Knight". c. 1245.

Fig. 227. Stowe-nine-churches (Northants). Purbeck marble reclining "Knight". c. 1260.

The two knights we illustrate in Figs. 223 and 224 appear to date from about 1245. The first (Fig. 223) was well preserved and needed little repair. The legs are crossed high up, a convention which became the standard pose for English knightly effigies for the next hundred years. The popular belief that these cross-legged knights were Crusaders is obviously untenable; it was no doubt introduced merely to give a certain liveliness of effect, and is a purely English feature, which never occurs in French monumental effigies, though it had been frequent in the statues of the twelfth-century Toulouse school. The Temple knight is wearing a steel cap with protection for the face and chin which is left smooth and is therefore not meant for mail. The hands are crossed on the breast and a cushion placed under the head. The second knight (Fig. 224) needed heavier repairs, but the easy attitude and spreading of the tail of the surcoat over the slab show that the sculptor was at last attempting to realise the recumbent position, and the coal-scuttle helmet gives an individuality to this figure.

Outside London we may illustrate the straight-legged type by a fine effigy at Sandwich (Fig. 225) with shield laid on breast, and a bold canopy over his head. About the middle of the century a more restless type comes into favour: not only is the warrior represented with crossed legs, but he is drawing his sword from the sheath, as though he were not dead, but just about to start up from slumber to engage a foe. A knight in a closed visor at Walkerne (Fig. 226) is an early example of this attitude, c. 1245, and later ones may be found in the second Longespée at Salisbury, Wareham, Winchelsea, Rushton and elsewhere. The quieter type was being produced at the same time, side by side with these vigorous warriors, as at Stowe-nine-churches (Fig. 227), where hands are laid one on the breast and the other at the side, and the surcoat is spread out on the slab as in the Temple knight with the coal-scuttle helmet.

The latest of the Purbeck knights is probably that at Dodford (Fig. 228). Here the attitude is rather quieter, though the sword-drawing motive is still employed. It is tempting to connect the quiet type of these knights with the marblers working for the king at Westminster, where the restful, more sculpturesque design was favoured, and the livelier sword-drawing figures with some other workshop, possibly that of Salisbury or of the quarries at Corfe itself, though this, of course, must be purely a conjecture.

A few ladies have come down to us from the Purbeck shops, though not of the earliest period. One at Worcester (Fig. 230), c. 1240, has a long robe spread over her feet without any attempt to indicate the prone position, though she is given a pillow under her head. She wears a wimple under her chin, and the slab beneath is ornamented with undercut foliage. Romsey has a lady, c. 1270 (Fig. 231), under a bold canopy, with foliated sides to the slab. She is holding up the folds of her dress with one hand and fingering the cord of her cloak with the other, very much in the attitude of the later Wells statues or the Virgin from Westminster chapter-house.

Civilians wear a long plain gown, as at Winchelsea, and we have one royal effigy in Purbeck marble. Our earliest Norman kings were buried in Normandy, and the effigies of Henry II and his queen and of Richard I at Fontevrault[1] are quite different in style from anything we have in England. The Purbeck effigy, therefore, of King John at Worcester is the earliest of the long series of royal tombs in England.[2] It looks some years later than his death in 1216, being boldly carved in high relief with well-executed drapery (Fig. 229). Two small figures of bishops are carved on each side of his head, representing St Oswald and St Wulfstan, between whose shrines the wicked king was buried in the hope that under their escort his soul might obtain a better reception than was justified by his life![3]

[1] See the author's *Medieval Sculpture in France*, Figs. 354, 355, and Stothard's drawings.
[2] William Rufus was buried at Winchester, but the tower fell on the grave. The coped slab shown as his tomb is a very doubtful identification.
[3] King John's effigy seems to have preserved much of its original colour when drawn by Stothard, but it was unfortunately gilded all over by order of Queen Victoria. It has now been cleaned and polished, but has necessarily lost the old colouring.

Fig. 228. Dodford (Northants). The latest Purbeck marble "Knight". c. 1305.

Fig. 229. Worcester. Presbytery. Purbeck marble effigy of King John. c. 1230.

Fig. 230. Worcester. Lady Chapel. Purbeck marble effigy of "Lady". *c.* 1240.

Fig. 231. Romsey. Transept. Purbeck marble effigy of "Lady". *c.* 1270.

Fig. 232. Ryton. Frosterley marble "Deacon".

Fig. 233. Lichfield. Grey stone "Bishop", probably *c.* 1245.

Fig. 234. Pershore. Freestone "Knight". *c.* 1280.

As already pointed out, the products of the Purbeck marblers set the standard for tomb-making for most of the thirteenth century. Substitutes were found for the genuine article in places where it was not available, such as the Frosterley marble in Durham, which is bluer in colour and has much larger shells. An effigy of a deacon holding a book at Ryton (Fig. 232) is in this material, and has the bold lines and smooth broad folds of the later Purbeck school. At Lichfield a bishop in a kind of dark slaty limestone is probably to be assigned to Bishop Patteshull (1239–41) and is based on the Purbeck style of the middle of the century (Fig. 233), while at

194

Fig. 235. Abergavenny. Chancel. Freestone effigy of "Lady". c. 1270.

Fig. 236. Exeter. Lady Chapel. Freestone effigy of "Bishop Bronescombe". c. 1280.

13-2

Worcester, beside the Purbeck bishop we have illustrated (Fig. 215), there is an obvious copy in a softer freestone which has worn away more severely, but must have been a little coarser in treatment. Bishop Aquablanca, c. 1270, at Hereford, is based on the type of Archbishop de Gray at York, and a large number of freestone knights, such as that at Pershore (Fig. 234), owe much to the later Purbeck models. A striking effigy of a lady at Abergavenny with a shield blazoned with fleur-de-lys resting on her breast (Fig. 235) is also just what we should expect to have found in a marble prototype. A knight at Bridport has traces of having been painted black, as though in imitation of the marble.

Local schools existed in various parts of the country, such as that of Bristol and the Doulting quarries which has already been described, but most of them do not become very important till quite the end of the century, when they will fall better into place in a later chapter.

The distinguished figure of Bishop Bronescombe, d. 1280, at Exeter, is based on the later Purbeck models, but begins to show a distinct advance in the treatment of the drapery with thin overlapping folds (Fig. 236). The head is raised high on a double cushion, and the little leaves carved on the canopy begin to assume the naturalistic form of the last years of the century, and proclaim this effigy as transitional to the next period with which we have to deal.

Chapter V

THE FOURTEENTH CENTURY
(OR DECORATED PERIOD)

STATUES; ARCHITECTURAL AND FURNITURE SCULPTURE

It has been already pointed out in our introductory chapter that by the second half of the thirteenth century there are signs that the sculptors of figure and foliage were beginning to specialise. The Purbeck marblers were sending out tombs and effigies ready carved, besides shafts and capitals, and we have seen how in 1258 John of St Albans is spoken of as "sculptor of the king's images". These imagers of the end of the thirteenth century no doubt began as masons, and their work shows a sympathy for their architectural surroundings and a dignified monumental style which attains the high-water mark of medieval art. By the beginning of the fourteenth century, however, we begin to see signs of the divorce of the figure-sculpture from the building craft. The imager has become a specialist and begins to let individual dexterities and clever fancies lure him away from the monumental ideal. The result is that in spite of greater knowledge and surer technique there is a loss of dignity and his work merits such descriptions as "pretty" and "graceful" rather than "grand" or "noble". The change comes slowly, and is perhaps less noticeable in the tomb-sculpture than in the architectural work.

Just at the turning point we have the famous Eleanor Crosses, the accounts for which fortunately survive, and, as already stated (see p. 14), were published in *Archaeologia* in 1842. The surviving crosses are those at Waltham and Hardingstone, just outside Northampton. There is also a smaller cross, not mentioned in the accounts, at Geddington in Northamptonshire, which has suffered less from restoration than the others. Alexander of Abingdon's statues at Waltham,

Fig. 238. Hardingstone (Northampton).
"Queen Eleanor" on Cross. *c.* 1292.

Fig. 237. Waltham. The "Eleanor"
of the Cross. *c.* 1292.

of which we show the best preserved, are not portraits in the modern sense, but seem based on the model set by images of the Virgin or other female saints (Fig. 237). The queen stands with body slightly bent and the weight resting on one leg; one hand plays with the cord of her cloak as in the Wells statues, and the cloak falls in a cascade of little twisted folds at the side. It is, perhaps, worth while to draw attention to the likeness of these statues to a beautiful effigy of a lady at Aldworth (Fig. 239), not very far from Abingdon, which exhibits very much the same treatment, and it is tempting to suggest that this is another work of Alexander's, or at any rate came from the same atelier in which he was trained.

William of Ireland's statues at Northampton show a change in style, though still based on the Virgin motive. The drapery is brought across the figure in flatter and more sweeping folds (Fig. 238). William is described indifferently as mason (*caementarius*) and imager (*imaginator*), which seems to prove that architectural grounding of his craft which we have claimed for the thirteenth-century sculptors. There is a general resemblance of some of these statues to the tomb of Aveline, Countess of Lancaster, d. 1273, in Westminster Abbey (Fig. 240), and we may therefore take these together as typical productions of the London workshops in the last decade of the thirteenth century. The first signs of this thin and fluttering drapery may have appeared at Salisbury on the west front, where the decayed fragments which remain seem to indicate a departure from the Wells style which we should have expected to see developing in a façade evidently based on the Wells model. Possibly suggestions from France of a more elegant treatment may have begun to exercise some influence by this time.

The Geddington Eleanors are less distinguished, though better preserved (Fig. 241). They too have the cascade of the folds of the cloak at the sides, but the coarser rendering seems to be more local work, based on the statues of the Lincoln or Peterborough school.

Fig. 239. Aldworth (Berks). The "Lady" effigy. c. 1300.

Fig. 240. Westminster. "Aveline, Countess of Lancaster", d. 1273. Effigy probably c. 1290.

Fig. 241. Geddington Cross.
"Queen Eleanor."

Fig. 242. Lichfield. South side of choir.
c. 1300.

The one remaining ancient statue on one of the buttresses at Lichfield (Fig. 242) bears a strong resemblance to the Eleanor statues. The same arrangement of the draperies with folds of the cloak at the side can be seen repeated, but the long hair falling on each side of the face in zigzag curls is a regular feature of early fourteenth-century style, especially in the Midlands and North.

On the other hand, the rather florid style of the Lincoln angels with the smooth baggy folds is continued in a more or less exaggerated form at Durham in two angels placed high up near the vault at the junction of the choir with the eastern transept known as the Nine Altars (Fig. 243). These must be dated *c.* 1280.

The exaggerations in attitude and hair treatment, which we see beginning in the Durham angels, are carried a little farther in the Madonna of the York chapter-house (Fig. 244), *c.* 1300. The pronounced sway of the figure, the corkscrew curls and voluminous folds over the feet are characteristic of the florid style encouraged by the deep-bedded magnesian limestone from Tadcaster, as we shall see when we come to deal with the effigies of this period. There seems to be more affinity to German sculpture at York than at Westminster, where French suggestions seem favoured, though both schools retain their own individuality. The rather narrow sloping shoulders of this type are repeated in some headless statues now in the Minster Library at York and in the collection of much worn figures at Howden (Figs. 245, 246), though these last are more restrained and form a half-way house towards the statues of the eastern midlands. A priest and a St John holding a long scroll are among the best preserved, and a Synagogue, a St Peter and a St Paul have the swaying attitude referred to above.

The range of hills stretching across Northamptonshire, Rutland and Lincolnshire provides excellent building stone, of which the coarse oolite of Barnack and the finer variety quarried at Ancaster were most famous. This region has a fine series of churches, which frequently make use of figure work. Some statues on the Abbot's

Fig. 243. Durham. Choir.

Fig. 244. York. Chapter-house.
Madonna of doorway. *c.* 1300.

Fig. 245. Howden. "Priest" in south
transept. *c.* 1320.

Fig. 246. Howden. "St John"
in choir-screen. *c.* 1320.

gate-house at Peterborough, of which we show the "Prior" (Fig. 247), may serve to start the series as they date from the last years of the thirteenth century. The high shoulders, raised arms and straight folds distinguish them from the swaying figures and billowy draperies of York. The figure of St John in a richly decorated niche on the tower at Heckington church (Fig. 248) is a good example of a few years later, *c.* 1320. This is still mason's work, probably done by the same man who carved the foliage of the ogee-headed canopy and the fine gargoyles on either side. A number of external statues survive in this district, such as the Madonna on a bracket on the north side of the nave at Boston (Fig. 249), or the big seated figure of Christ at Swynnerton, Staffs (Fig. 250), which must have come from an exterior niche, probably in the gable of some important building. This last is some eight or nine feet high, and it is suggested that it may have come from Lichfield, though there seems to be no record of how it got to its present location. The long body is evidently meant to correct the perspective as seen from below, and the hair treatment is what we have noted elsewhere at this period.

A number of statues of varying quality may be found in positions high up on these churches. They are mostly weather-worn, but naturally lack the finish of the porch statues of Lincoln. They are well suited to their position and often pleasing in effect, but as a rule fall a little short of the dignity of those of the preceding generation.

But it is in the internal fittings, screens and tombs that we find the most characteristic works of the fourteenth century. The great church-building era was drawing to a close, and the imagers were called upon to supply figure-work for the internal fittings. In these we find a delicacy and fancy and technical skill on a higher level than ever, though the smaller scale leads to a less monumental treatment. A transitional figure of St Christopher at Terrington St Clement (Fig. 262) seems too delicately wrought for an external

Fig. 247. Peterborough. Gateway.
"Prior." *c.* 1290.

Fig. 248. Heckington. Statue on south side
of tower. *c.* 1320.

Fig. 249. Boston. "Madonna" on
north side of nave. *c*. 1340.

Fig. 250. Swynnerton.
Colossal statue.

Fig. 251. Beverley. Canopy of Percy Tomb. _c._ 1330.

position; the smooth draperies and general treatment point to a date in the second half of the fourteenth century.

In this line the masterpiece of the York imagers was the tomb erected at Beverley for Lady Eleanor Percy, who died in 1328 (Fig. 251). Some doubt has been felt as to the identification, as one of the shields carved on it bears the arms of England quartered with those of France (Fig. 253) which was not adopted by Edward III before 1339, but such an elaborate monument may easily have taken several years to complete. There is no effigy: possibly this was a brass, but the slab at the bottom may have been tampered with. The wonderful canopy wrought in the magnesian limestone from Tadcaster is almost perfect. At the top is a statue of Christ seated receiving in a napkin the soul of the deceased, and large statues of angels on either side are supported by brackets composed of grotesque figures (Fig. 255). The cusps of the ogee arch are occupied by knights and a lady holding shields carved with heraldic devices, and other spaces are occupied by little figures, angels and heads. A corbel below has a

Fig. 252. Beverley Minster. Corbel from Percy Tomb. _c._ 1330.

Fig. 253. Beverley. Percy Tomb. Detail.

most spirited combat between a lion and dragon, which combines the vigour of such an old Romanesque carving as that in the York museum (Fig. 110) with the refined skill of a later age (Fig. 252). In the large statues we recognise the sloping shoulders, billowy drapery and side curls of the York school, and though the monumental conception of the previous generation is not quite reached we can forgive the slight loss of dignity when we contemplate the exquisite finish and masterly handling of every detail.[1]

Corresponding work of the Ancaster school may be found in the Easter sepulchres in which the Host was reserved from Good Friday till Easter Day. Usually these were temporary erections, but in Lincolnshire and the neighbouring district they were permanent stone erections, and in such churches as Heckington and Hawton their elaborate carving corresponding to that of the sedilia on the opposite side gave a very sumptuous appearance to the chancel (Fig. 256). In the centre there is a relief of the Resurrection of Our

Fig. 254. Lincoln Cathedral. "Easter Sepulchre." *c.* 1300.

[1] The back of the screen at Southwell has more delicate work of this type. The fragments of St William's shrine in the York museum, and seated headless figures dug up at Fountains and Rievaulx, are other examples of the northern imagers' work of this period.

Fig. 255. Beverley. "Angel"
on Percy Tomb. *c.* 1330.

Fig. 256. Hawton (Notts). "Easter Sepulchre."
c. 1330.

Fig. 257. Gosberton (Lincs). Spandrel of tomb. *c.* 1310.

Lord, and the sleeping soldiers are carved at the bottom of the monument, and there is a striking group of the Ascension at the top. The whole effect tends to be over-elaborate and crowded with a consequent loss of dignity. The Easter sepulchre in Lincoln Cathedral is a little earlier, *c.* 1300, and the sleeping soldiers must have been very fine before mutilation (Fig. 254).[1] A tomb at Gosberton has some very pleasing angels swinging censers over its canopy (Fig. 257), which also come from the same workshops, as also did slabs at Mattersey representing the Invention of the Cross and a St Martin dividing his cloak (Fig. 258), which must have formed part of an altar piece.

[1] Other sculptured Easter sepulchres remain at Navenby and Fledborough, and a less dignified one at Patrington in Yorkshire.

213

Fig. 258. Mattersey (Notts). "St Martin." *c.* 1310.

The cloister door at Norwich has niches carved round its head containing figures of early fourteenth-century date, which have many of the characteristics of those we have been examining (Fig. 259). Our illustration shows Christ at the top, a charming angel, a pope (who is supposed to be Aaron corresponding to Moses on the other side) and John the Baptist in his robe of camel's hair. The most ambitious monument of the first half of the fourteenth century in the eastern counties is the Lady Chapel at Ely, begun in 1321 and

Fig. 259. Norwich Cathedral. Doorway into cloister. *c.* 1300.

finished in 1349. It is surrounded by an arcade of marvellous intricacy, with statuettes standing or sitting under the projecting ogee canopies, and the spandrels filled with reliefs illustrating the life and miracles of the Virgin.[1] These must have originally numbered over a hundred, but many have been cut away and all so badly mutilated that hardly a head remains. The work is in a chalk-stone (clunch) which is easy to work and tempts the carver to over elaboration of detail. There are exaggerations of gesture, and certain features like hands are sometimes too large in the desire to make the story dramatic, but the whole effect when new and gleaming with colour and gold must have been overwhelming (Fig. 260).

Coming south we have in the base of the shrine at St Albans a last *tour de force* on the part of the Purbeck marblers, who after this seem to have abandoned the attempt to compete with workers in less obstinate materials in figure-work. It was discovered in 1872 in more than 2000 fragments, and was carefully pieced together like a jig-saw puzzle. The spandrels are occupied by seated kings and censing angels, and at the east end in the gable is the martyrdom of the saint (Fig. 261). This last is awkwardly crowded into the space, but the bigger figures are graceful, and the naturalistic foliage of the first decade of the century is deeply undercut and must have required extraordinary skill to execute.

Perhaps the most accomplished work of the southern imagers is to be found in the chapter doorway at Rochester. There are statues of the Church and Synagogue on either side, the latter with bandaged eyes, broken staff and the Tables of the Law falling from her hand (Fig. 263). The Church has a new head which replaces an absurd male head affixed in a previous restoration. The smooth thin draperies with overlapping folds are typical of the new manner which had come in with the second quarter of the century. Finer still, and less touched

---

[1] These have been elucidated as far as their condition allows by Dr M. R. James, *The Sculptures in the Lady Chapel at Ely*, 1895.

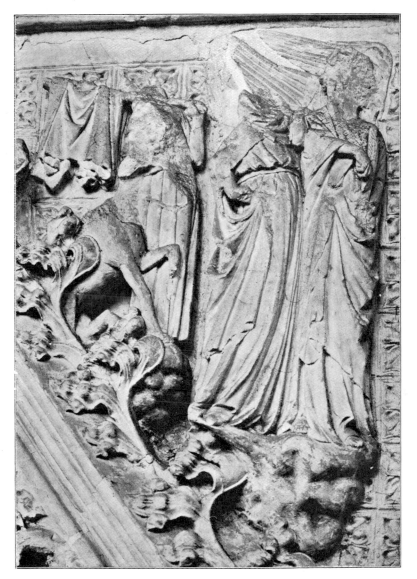

Fig. 260. Ely Cathedral. Relief in Lady Chapel. "Journey of the Virgin to Bethlehem." *c.* 1340.

Fig. 261. St Albans. The shrine. "The Martyrdom of St Alban."
c. 1306.

up, are four seated figures of Doctors of the Church (or Evangelists?)
occupying broad niches in the mouldings of the door-head. Their
furrowed faces, deep-set eyes, and whole pose as they sit in front of
their reading desks, are those of an individual pictorial expression,
such as an image-maker, as opposed to a building mason, would
cultivate (Fig. 264). Work of the same school, if not of the same
hand, may be seen in the exquisite little groups of monks at their
meals (Fig. 265) and at their desks in the trefoils of the canopy over
Archbishop Meopham's tomb (d. 1333). They have the same bold
head-features and broad smooth draperies with twisted folds at the
edges, which we found at Rochester.

218

Fig. 262. Terrington St Clement.
"St Christopher" in tower. *c.* 1340.

Fig. 263. Rochester. Chapter doorway.
"Synagogue." *c.* 1330.

Fig. 264. Rochester. Chapter doorway. *c.* 1330.

There are some broken figures and one or two fine heads (Fig. 266) from a destroyed screen or altar piece at Cobham, Kent, which are good examples of what was being produced by the imagers of this period, and at Winchester there are some fine heads, of which we illustrate one which has the romantic hair treatment of fourteenth-century style (Fig. 267), though this may possibly be a later survival. There are also some headless statues, three or four feet high, from a screen or reredos which are excellent examples of the new style of

220

Fig. 265. Canterbury. Abp. Meopham's tomb (d. 1333).

Fig. 266. Cobham (Kent). Image-head.
c. 1320.

Fig. 267. Winchester. Head in feretory.

Fig. 268. Winchester.   Fig. 269. Winchester. "Madonna." *c.* 1340.

drapery (Fig. 268), with silky overlappings and composed of a thin almost transparent material showing something of the figure and limbs beneath. The swaying pose is a little theatrical and shows a tendency to the picturesque which is characteristic of the first half of the fourteenth century. Winchester also possesses the upper part of a statue of the Madonna which was probably an altar image (Fig. 269). It has very smooth draperies and a charming expression, helped out by considerable remains of colour.[1]

[1] The globe has now been removed as it is not considered genuine.

Fig. 271. Westminster. Canopy of Aymer de Valence's
Tomb. *c.* 1323.

Fig. 270. Westminster. Canopy of Crouchback's
Tomb. *c.* 1296.

For the Westminster style we must turn to the magnificent tombs in the sanctuary of the Abbey. The statues which formerly crowned the canopies have gone, but the trefoils at the head of the arch have carvings of the deceased princes on horseback, which resemble the figures on the fine seals of the period (Figs. 270, 271). The three tombs in question are those of Edmund Crouchback, Earl of Lancaster, d. 1296; of Aveline his wife, d. *c.* 1273; and, between them, of Aymer de Valence, Earl of Pembroke, d. 1323. In the little trefoils it is interesting to compare the quiet stately figure of 1296 with the

Fig. 272. Westminster. The tomb-chest of the Earl of Lancaster
(d. 1296).

Fig. 273. Westminster. The tomb-chest of Aymer de Valence (d. 1323).

galloping, flashy but less satisfying horseman of thirty years later. The weepers, too, as the little figures of relatives or mourners ranged along the tomb-chest are called, also show a decline in art from the stately little figures in the drapery of the Eleanor Crosses on Crouchback's tomb (Figs. 272, 274) to the tighter dresses and smoother and more monotonous folds of those on Aymer's monument (Fig. 273). It is interesting to compare these with the weepers of Prince John of Eltham's tomb, also in the Abbey, d. 1334, which mark a further step in the direction of theatrical exaggeration and picturesque poses (Fig. 275). These are in alabaster, cut out and set against a background of dark stone or marble, and the introduction of this new material leads us on to the new movement which plays such an important part in the story of the last Gothic period, to which we shall return in a subsequent chapter.

Fig. 274. Westminster. Weepers from Crouchback Monument.

Fig. 275. Westminster. The alabaster weeper of John of Eltham (d. 1334).

Churches in the district supplied by the Ancaster and neighbouring quarries were decorated with a profusion of carving of figures as well as foliage. Heckington church, a building of quite modest size, had besides its Easter sepulchre and sedilia, and besides 31 niches for statues, no less than 80 separate carvings of heads and figures on corbels inside and out, and as many as 198 gargoyles (Fig. 276), many of them of large size. In these the mason was able to give free play to his fancy, and towers and parapets all over the country bear witness to the way he took advantage of his opportunity, though the exposed position has often led to decay and, what is worse, to

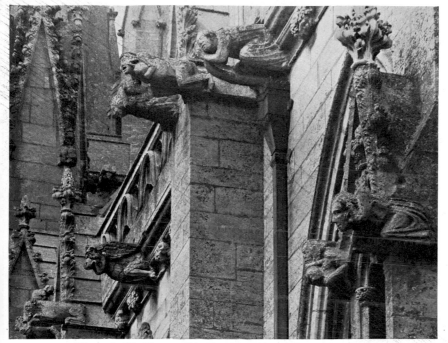

Fig. 276. Heckington (Lincs). Gargoyles of chancel. *c.* 1330.

restoration. Good examples of mid-century date may be found on the nave and fine south porch at Over, near Cambridge (Figs. 277, 278). These continued to be popular to the end of the Gothic era, and examples are so numerous that a book could be devoted to them alone, but these few must suffice in a general work like the present.

A group of churches in Oxfordshire and neighbouring districts developed a special style of their own, with long cornices under the eaves carved with heads, animals, hunting scenes and monsters. Those at Adderbury (Fig. 279), Stannion, Hanwell, Alkerton and Olney may be mentioned. In these, too, capitals are formed of crouching human or grotesque figures, which take the place of foliage, as at Hanwell (Fig. 280).

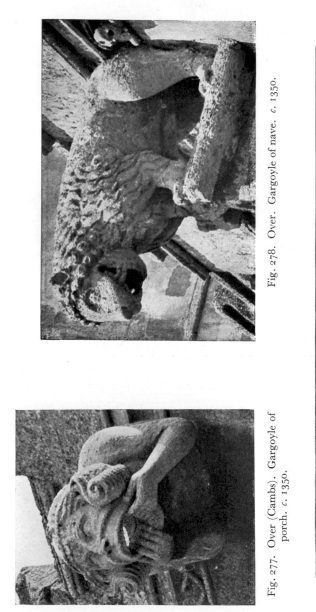

Fig. 277. Over (Cambs). Gargoyle of porch. *c.* 1350.

Fig. 278. Over. Gargoyle of nave. *c.* 1350.

Fig. 279. Adderbury (Oxon). Cornice of nave. *c.* 1340.

Fig. 280. Hanwell (Oxon). Capital of nave. *c.* 1340.

The use of heads as stops and corbels continues, and we have an astonishing variety of expression and liveliness. Examples may be taken from Wells chapter-house, where colour adds life to the smile on the face of the pope (Fig. 281), Exeter (Fig. 282), Winchelsea, where the elaborate corkscrew side-curls of the period are well represented (Fig. 284), and Ely, where king, queen, bishop and prior— the latter usually identified as Alan of Walsingham, the sacrist who is given the credit for designing the famous octagon—are placed as a kind of signature to their work on the building (Fig. 283). Round

Fig. 281. Wells. Chapter-house.
Head of "Pope". *c.* 1310.

Fig. 282. Exeter.
c. 1290.

the octagon at Ely are a series of corbels carved with incidents from the life of St Etheldreda (Fig. 285). Though skilfully carved and full of charm when regarded individually in detail, they are not sufficiently bold to be really effective in their position on the building. Corbels composed of grotesque figures mask the junction of arches, or conduct the vaulting shafts down to the capitals, as at Exeter. In the latter cathedral it is interesting to compare those of the choir of *c.* 1290 (Fig. 286), and their bold and effective relief and naturalistic foliage, with those of the nave of some 40 years later (Fig. 287) in which the proportions are more correct, but the cutting shallower and the whole effect colder and more confused.

Vaulting bosses assume more importance as the vaults grow more complicated. This again is a specially English development, as our comparatively low vaults with numerous extra ribs, and especially the lierne vaults of the middle of the century, gave far more opportunity

Fig. 283. Ely. "Alan of Walsingham."   Fig. 284. Winchelsea.

Fig. 285. Ely. The capitals of the central lantern.
The "Story of St Etheldreda". *c.* 1330.

Fig. 287. Exeter. Corbel in nave. *c.* 1330.

Fig. 286. Exeter. Corbel in choir. *c.* 1290.

Fig. 288. Chester. Boss in vault of chapter-house.
"Madonna and Child." *c.* 1260. (From cast.)

for the display of sculpture to cover the junctions and crossing places of the ribs than the lofty French vaults which were so high that any elaboration of this kind would have been ineffective from the floor. During the greater part of the thirteenth century bosses had been mainly of moderate size and usually confined themselves to foliage, but we have already (Fig. 149) described the splendid examples in the Muniment Room at Westminster, *c.* 1250. A very beautiful boss from the chapter-house at Chester (Fig. 288), *c.* 1260, may serve to carry on the story. There are some fine bosses of the end of the thirteenth century in the high vault of the choir at Exeter, which have the grace usually associated with sculpture of that date (Fig. 289). It is estimated that there are some 570 bosses in the vaults of Exeter Cathedral,[1] ranging from six inches in diameter up to nearly three

[1] *Bosses and Corbels of Exeter Cathedral*, by E. K. Prideaux and G. R. Holt Shafto, 1910.

Fig. 289. Exeter. Boss in choir.
c. 1290.

Fig. 290. Norwich. Cloister, east walk.
"Crucifixion." c. 1300.

feet for the great bosses of the ridge rib. The finest are those of the east end, c. 1300, while those of the nave of some forty or fifty years later show the same decline in artistic quality which we saw in the corbels in the same parts of the cathedral.

As we reach the middle of the century the bosses of the high vaults tend to become coarser and rougher in execution, as it was realised that fine work could not be appreciated from the ground. Those at Tewkesbury, for instance, where they illustrate the Nativity (Fig. 291) and Passion scenes with angels playing musical instruments in the less important positions, are effective but lacking in refinement when looked at with a magnifying glass, though this may partly be due to the thick coat of modern painting and gilding.[1]

[1] These have been minutely described and illustrated in "Roof bosses in the nave of Tewkesbury Abbey", by C. J. P. Cave, in *Archaeologia*, LXXIX, 1929. Mr Cave has devised a remarkable combination of telephoto lens and a spot light, which has enabled him to produce a wonderful collection of photographs of bosses, etc., situated in positions where they can hardly be appreciated by the naked eye. He has published photographs of the later bosses at Norwich in *Archaeologia*, LXXXIII, 1933.

Fig. 291. Tewkesbury. Boss in
nave-vault. *c.* 1350.

Fig. 292. Lincoln. Cloister.
Wooden boss. *c.* 1290.

It is, then, in the cloisters that we can look for the finest bosses
of this period, as they are not too highly placed to be seen, and were
therefore much more delicately wrought. There are some beautiful
wooden examples, *c.* 1290, in the cloister at Lincoln, of which we
show a bishop, possibly St Hugh (Fig. 292), carved in the best style
of the day. The cloisters at Norwich afford a particularly useful series
as the work was spread over 130 years, and three successive periods
can be studied side by side. The east walk was built *c.* 1300, and such
bosses as that of the Crucifixion (Fig. 290) have the charm of all the
lesser works of the time, the graceful swaying attitudes and naturalistic
foliage, and are quite in the tradition of the doorway already illustrated (see Fig. 259). The south walk followed about forty years later

Fig. 293. Norwich. Cloister. "The Son of Man."
c. 1340.

and illustrates the Apocalypse in a series of fine and dramatic scenes. The two examples given here are taken from Rev. i. 11–16 in which the Son of Man appears on his throne with the seven golden candlesticks, the seven stars in his right hand, and a two-edged sword proceeding out of his mouth (Fig. 293); and from Rev. viii. 8–9, "the second angel sounded, and as it were a great mountain burning with fire was cast into the sea...and the third part of the ships were destroyed" (Fig. 294). These are excellent examples of the simple and direct way in which a medieval carver tackled a subject which would have daunted any classical or modern artist; by so doing

Fig. 294. Norwich. Cloister. "The second Angel."
c. 1340.

he produces a graphic work of art, with the tremendous angel trumpeting above and all confusion below. Even here, however, some of the less successful bosses in their anecdotal and crowded compositions begin to pave the way for the more standardised uniformity of the fifteenth-century bosses of the west and north walks, the treatment of which must be postponed to a later chapter.[1]

[1] The Norwich bosses are now (1936) being cleaned and re-coloured under the advice of Prof. Tristram.

We have already had occasion to speak of the growing importance of funeral sculpture in dealing with the canopies and weepers of the tomb chests in such magnificent erections as the royal tombs at Westminster. It is now time to turn to the effigies[1] themselves.

It has been pointed out that the increasing use of painting sounded the death-knell of the Purbeck effigy, as it was found that softer and more easily worked stone, or even wood, produced very much the same effect when coated with paint, and details worked up in gesso, a kind of gummy plaster. For the next seventy or eighty years, therefore, from 1280 or 1290 to about 1360 the standard type of effigy is in freestone, until the lead is taken by the alabaster trade, which must be dealt with in our final chapter.

As in the building sculpture the quality of the stone available in the various districts will be found to be the determining factor of style, and though outside influences affect different centres in other ways, the material set before the tomb-maker must prove the basis of classification. Such classification must necessarily be vague with considerable overlapping of boundaries, and, as an effigy was a portable commodity, important tombs in the provinces may sometimes have been ordered from London or other leading centres, just as the Purbeck tombs had come from the quarries at Corfe. Still, allowing for these reservations, certain main schools, c. 1300 to c. 1360, may be distinguished, of which the south-western, northern, midland and London types are most important.

(a) The South-western Schools

As already seen, the Wells and Bristol effigies of the thirteenth century had formed a class by themselves which resisted to some extent the all-pervading influence of the Purbeck marblers. The fine oolite

---

[1] In this book the term "effigy" is reserved for the recumbent figure on a tomb, the upright standing figure being referred to as a "statue".

Fig. 295. Hereford. Lady Chapel. Oolite effigy of "Chancellor Swinfield". c. 1290.

Fig. 296. Exeter. North aisle of choir. "Knight" with squire, page and horse. c. 1320.

available allowed of delicate detail, but was not always very deep in bed, and there is therefore a tendency to keep the effigies fairly flat. The effigy of Chancellor Swinfield, *c.* 1290, at Hereford may be taken as a typical example (Fig. 295). The depressed chin, small features, hands and other projecting features kept low, and the draperies neatly laid in silky overlapping folds are characteristic, and appear in such figures as those attributed to Bishop Droxford, *c.* 1329, and Dean Myddleton, *c.* 1337, at Wells; Dean Aquablanca, *c.* 1320, at Hereford, etc.

Exeter, where a soft sandstone, or a big chalk-stone from Beer, was in use, produced figures of a much bolder and less refined type, like the knight with squire standing at his head and page and horse at his feet, in the cathedral (Fig. 296). He lies slightly on one side, shield on arm, with legs crossed and drawing his sword from the scabbard—a lively representation far removed from the original idea of a laid-out corpse. Less truculent attitudes are assumed by the knight and lady at Beer Ferrers (Fig. 297), and by the knights of the Berkeley family at Bristol, who clasp their hands in prayer (Fig. 298), in all of which London influence may be suspected.

In all these knights the mail and surcoat of the crusading period are retained, with a round steel cap usually worn over the mail coif. As we approach the middle of the century, the steel cap tends to become pointed and approaches in shape the bascinet of the French wars of the second half of the century. From about 1320 to 1340 the surcoat was often cut short in front, but left longer behind, in which form it has often erroneously been called the "cyclas". This was eventually replaced by the tight-fitting leather "jupon" reaching only to the hips, which is the characteristic feature of the Edwardian period. Towards 1340 or 1350 there was also a tendency to vary attitudes: thus at Abergavenny one knight has his legs straight instead of crossed and another called Lawrence de Hastings (Fig. 299) lies on one side in a graceful attitude with one hand on his breast as if asleep.

240

Fig. 297. Beer Ferrers Church (Devon). Freestone "Knight" and "Lady". *c.* 1300.

Fig. 298. Bristol. Choir-aisle. The cross-legged "Berkeley". *c.* 1300.

Fig. 299. Abergavenny. Freestone "Knight" called Lawrence de Hastings. *c.* 1340.

Fig. 301. Bradford-on-Avon. *c.* 1300.

Ladies, *c.* 1300 usually wear the wimple, frequently with a straight band across the forehead with a veil over it, as at Bradford-on-Avon (Fig. 301). Later, a round frilled cap begins to appear, though this hardly comes into fashion until the second half of the century.

(b) The Northern Schools

The big-blocked magnesian limestone from Tadcaster seems to have been the governing factor in the style of the York effigy makers, and the florid types evolved were copied as far as possible in the fine sandstones and other materials available in the North. We may take the knight and lady at Bedale (Fig. 300) as typical of their productions. In these the surcoat of the knight is voluminous and the lady's skirts fall about her feet in billowy convolutions. The knight is bareheaded with side curls, and the mail coif thrown back; a depressed ogee canopy comes close over the head. The mail also is rendered in interlacing rings instead of in the parallel ridges usual in the South, and hands are folded in prayer. Sword-belts and other accessories are profusely ornamented, and the whole effect florid and bold as

Fig. 302. London. Temple Church. Yorkshire "Knight". *c.* 1300.

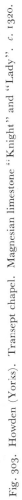

Fig. 303. Howden (Yorks). Transept chapel. Magnesian limestone "Knight" and "Lady". *c.* 1320.

Fig. 304. Alnwick. Effigy of "Lady". *c.* 1330.

compared with the quiet, sober and refined work of the Bristol imagers. The effigies are laid flat on their backs with no sign of the half-sideway reclining posture seen in London and the South. The head and mail treatment can be well seen in an effigy in the Temple Church, London, said by Richardson, who restored[1] the Temple figures, to have been brought in about 1682 from Kirkham Abbey in Yorkshire (Fig. 302). Other very similar examples occur at Fountains and at Howden (Fig. 303). In the latter the lady beside her husband shows her legs crossed beneath her flowing gown—a very unusual attitude in a female figure.

Farther North a rather simpler type of lady was evolved with smoother draperies, but still under the depressed ogee canopy. There is an excellent example at Alnwick (Fig. 304) and a very similar

[1] He reported the effigy in fairly good condition, but had to renew the nose, the right lock of hair, part of the shield, and some of the more exposed parts of the mail which were worn.

Fig. 305. Threckingham (Lincs). Ancaster "Knight" and "Lady". c. 1310.

Fig. 306. Gosberton (Lincs). Ancaster "Knight". c. 1310.

Fig. 307. Gonalston. Effigy of "Lady". *c.* 1310.

figure at Staindrop. These ladies clasp hands in prayer and wear a
wimple under the chin and a veil over the head, giving a triangular
aperture for the face.

In the Ancaster district a more sober presentation usually prevails,
influenced perhaps to some extent by London types. The hands are
usually folded in prayer and the mail with interlacing rings is mostly
favoured, but the mail coif usually covers the head, with or without a
steel cap, and the billowy folds of drapery are less pronounced. Good
examples occur at Threckingham and Gosberton (Figs. 305, 306). In
the latter the smoother folds of the surcoat and graceful attitude seem
to have come from the South, though the floral diaper work along the
plinth is reminiscent of Lincoln. At Gonalston, Notts, a very beautiful
lady retains the canopy, though of loftier proportions than those of
Yorkshire, and ornamented with stiff-leaf foliage on one side and
naturalistic on the other (Fig. 307). She is holding a small pot or
reliquary in her clasped hands, and her draperies are more those of
Madonna statues, apart from her head-dress of more fashionable
type. They may derive from Purbeck models, such as the lady at

Fig. 308. Ledbury. Effigy of "Priest". *c.* 1330.

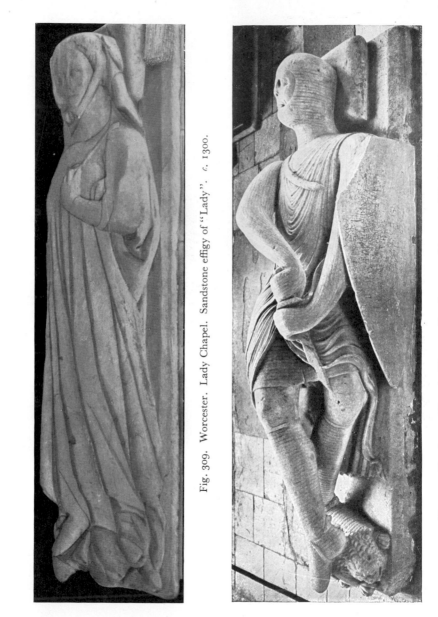

Fig. 309. Worcester. Lady Chapel. Sandstone effigy of "Lady". c. 1300.

Fig. 310. Dorchester (Oxon). Vigorous London type of freestone "Knight". c. 1310.

Romsey (see Fig. 231). It is worth noting that at Ancaster itself some unfinished effigies with the main outlines merely roughed out are preserved in the church porch, showing that it was the practice, at any rate in some instances, to prepare these tomb figures on the actual site of the quarry, as had been done at Corfe before, and was afterwards done at Chellaston where the alabaster was found.

(c) *The Midland and London Schools*

As we approach the capital city we find its influence spreading and affecting local productions, and as stone-carvers seem to have travelled fairly extensively and their wares were also portable it becomes more difficult to separate the work of the different districts. Round Lichfield, Coventry and Chester a rather coarse sandstone was the usual material, and as this did not allow of the incisive cutting of the Bristol oolite we find effigies bluntly rendered, and depending for their effect on the gesso finishing, which has in most cases perished. Our examples, therefore, like the Worcester lady in Fig. 309, look rough and uninteresting in their present condition, as we have to supply mentally the details which made them attractive.

A priest at Ledbury (Fig. 308) may serve as a second example. He is set in a niche with shafts, and apart from the cushion under his head he really looks best set up on end against the wall, as he is at present, there being few concessions to the recumbent attitude.

In Northamptonshire types approach those of the Ancaster district or follow the Eleanor Cross tradition for the ladies, but most of the South country looked to London as the centre of fashion. Two of the later knights in the Temple are in Reigate stone, but follow closely on the Purbeck models, though some of these stone figures tend to exaggerate the liveliness of the later Purbeck knights, and are drawing their swords in a most determined manner. A knight at Dorchester, Oxon, may be taken as one representative of this vigorous type (Fig. 310), but there was also another type of a much more restful

Fig. 311. Westminster. Sanctuary. The "Earl of Lancaster", "Crouchback". *c.* 1296.

Fig. 312. Westminster. Sanctuary. The "Earl of Pembroke", Aymer de Valence. *c.* 1333.

Fig. 313. Oxford. Freestone "Ecclesiastic". c. 1320.

Fig. 314. Winchelsea (Sussex). The first "Alard". c. 1300.

character, with hands clasped in prayer. The royal effigies at Westminster adopt this fashion, and those of the Earl of Lancaster (Crouchback), d. 1296 (Fig. 311), and Aymer de Valence, Earl of Pembroke, d. 1323 (Fig. 312), lie in a quiet restful attitude, turned slightly to one side, with little angels seated at their heads which are supported by double cushions. The mail is not carved in the stone and must have been added in the gesso finish. The Countess of Lancaster's effigy has already been referred to for comparison with the Eleanor statues. Some boldly carved ecclesiastics, like Bishop Marcia at Wells, Bishop Leophard at Chichester and Prior Alexander de Sutton at Oxford (Fig. 313), do not quite fall in with the general sequence of the locally produced figures, and as the former two have the Westminster angels at the head they were probably direct importations from the capital. The same is probably the case with the fine Alard knight at Winchelsea (Fig. 314), lying under a gorgeous canopy in very much the Westminster pose, while a second knight in the same church seems a local copy of the model imported from London.

Fig. 315. Warkworth (Northants). Whitestone "Knight". *c.* 1350.

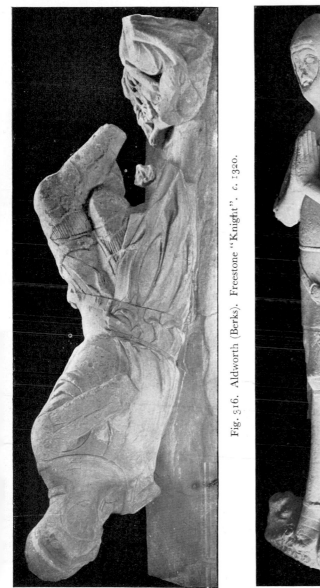

Fig. 316. Aldworth (Berks). Freestone "Knight". c. 1320.

Fig. 317. Ifield (Sussex). Caen stone "Knight" in chancel. c. 1335.

Fig. 318. Reepham (Norfolk). The "Kerdeston" Knight. c. 1350.

In all these military effigies we still have the mail and surcoat equipment, but as we approach 1350 a change begins to be felt, and there is also some attempt to give more variety of attitude, just as we found it in the West in the Abergavenny knights (see Fig. 299). At Aldworth, for instance, a knight of *c.* 1320, carved with great attention to detail, is resting on one arm as though wounded, almost in the attitude of the "Dying Gaul" of Pergamene art (Fig. 316). At Ifield (Fig. 317), Waterperry and in South Kensington Museum, there are knights with clasped hands and crossed legs which begin to show the change in accoutrements towards those of the next period. These knights of *c.* 1330–40 wear the short-fronted surcoat, and the steel cap is becoming pointed— almost a bascinet. The upper part of the surcoat is very smooth, as though composed of a thicker material, like leather. This must certainly be the case in a knight at Warkworth (Fig. 315) carved in a fine-grained white stone which allows of elaborate detail, as in the rosettes and lion-heads of the sword-belt; the lacing-up at the side of the leather coat is well shown. This garment seems to end in a kind of softer tail, like the short-fronted surcoat, and is well on the way to the close-fitting jupon of the next period. The arms also appear to be protected by plate instead of mail, and roundels with lion-heads protect the elbow. This fine figure also has the Westminster angels supporting the head.

Several romantic effigies of the second quarter of the fourteenth century depart in some particulars from the stock models. Thus at Ingham and Reepham (Fig. 318) in Norfolk knights are lying on a bed of stones, with large and formidable lions at their feet. In both of these the bascinet with "camail", or curtain of mail, suspended from it to protect the neck, indicate a date not far short of 1350.

Besides the freestone effigies we have figures in bronze, wood, and at the end of the period in alabaster. Although the first alabasters strictly belong to this chapter, it will be convenient to treat them all together in a later section.

Fig. 319. Westminster. "William de Valence", d. 1296. Effigy of oak plated with bronze and Limoges enamel.

One of the earliest of our metal effigies is that of William de Valence, d. 1296, half-brother of Henry III, in Westminster Abbey (Fig. 319). This was produced by affixing bronze plates to a wooden core, and adding the heraldry and ornaments in Limoges enamel. The effigy of Blanche de Champagne in the Louvre[1] is produced in exactly the same way, and we must therefore regard our tomb as a direct importation from Limoges.

The two magnificent bronze, or laton, effigies of Henry III (Fig. 320) and Queen Eleanor (Fig. 322) in the Abbey were made in London, as the accounts describe the ordering of the material for casting them after the king had approved the pattern submitted to him by Master William Torel, goldsmith (*aurifaber*) of London in 1291 and 1292.

They appear to have been cast on the cire-perdue system, in which a layer of wax is modelled upon a core, and then melted out and replaced by metal. They are unduly solid, as though Torel were used to smaller objects and these full-sized figures were new to him. The cushions and accessories are finely engraved with patterns similar

[1] See the author's *Medieval Sculpture in France*, Fig. 361.

Fig. 320. Westminster. Confessor's Chapel. Bronze effigy of Henry III. *c.* 1292.

Fig. 321. Canterbury. Transept. Wooden effigy of Archbishop Peckham. d. 1292.

Fig. 322. Westminster. Confessor's Chapel. Bronze head of "Queen Eleanor".
c. 1292.

to those worked in gesso on the stone and wood figures. The queen's head is raised on a double cushion, and her hair falls loose about her shoulders. Her features and arched eyebrows are those of the Madonna statues, and are an idealised version of a beautiful queen rather than an accurate portrait. The same must be said of Henry III's face as the king had been dead for twenty years when the tomb was erected. The general conception of both figures is founded upon the style of the London effigy makers in stone or marble, and as the metal preserves its original surface we are fortunate in being able

260

Fig. 323. Abergavenny. Wooden effigy of "Knight". c. 1300.

Fig. 324. Gloucester. Wooden "Knight". c. 1290.

Fig. 325. Danbury (Essex). Wooden "Knight". *c.* 1300.

to base our ideas of the masterpieces of the finest period of our native art on such important and well-preserved examples.

Wooden knights, ladies and ecclesiastics were also being fabricated in the London workshops and elsewhere in considerable numbers. They are commonest in the eastern counties, where wood was plentiful and stone scarce, but they are found everywhere. Archbishop Peckham, d. 1292, is commemorated by a wooden effigy at Canterbury (Fig. 321), which follows closely the type worked out in stone or marble. The mitre is missing and was probably added in metal. Jewels or glass and enamels may have been inset, but the loss of the gesso ornaments makes it difficult to appreciate the effect of these wooden figures, especially when we have also to allow for the decay of the surface from which most of them have suffered. We may take as examples of the quiet knight effigies, based on the Westminster royal models, a fairly well-preserved figure at Abergavenny, *c.* 1300 (Fig. 323), and a knight of about the same date at Danbury in Essex (Fig. 325). Both wear mail and surcoat, the details of the mail no doubt having been added in gesso, the hands are clasped in prayer, and the head rests on a double cushion. The lively type of knight may be represented by the figure called Robert of Normandy at Gloucester (Fig. 324), which was obviously made about the end of the thirteenth century, though it has been touched up and re-painted in more modern times. The sword-drawing hand and high raised knee show that the wood-carver was inclined to make the most of the opportunities given him by his easily worked material.[1]

[1] A re-painted knight at Chew Magna may serve to give an idea of what effect these wooden figures were intended to produce.

Chapter VI

THE LATE GOTHIC OR PERPENDICULAR PERIOD

(1) GENERAL REMARKS

The terrible visitation of the Black Death in 1348/1349 profoundly modified social conditions in the country, and when active building began again it was under altered conditions and in a different spirit. The shortage of labour led to greater organisation of the building trade and necessitated greater mobility on the part of the masons. The result in architecture was the crystallisation of the romantic Decorated style into the stately and efficient Perpendicular. Local styles tended to be submerged, though some broad distinctions can be made between east and west. Conditions were beginning to approximate more nearly to those of more modern times, and contract-work was becoming a substitute for artistic creation.

The sculpture, under such conditions, was produced from stock patterns and began to lose its intimate connection with the building. The masons constructed niches for it, and provided gargoyles or angel cornices, but left the statues to be bought separately at a shop, and added or not as funds permitted. Tradition prevented gross incongruity, and the general effect was not unpleasing, but individually such figures became monotonous and less interesting than their predecessors. Quality varied less with locality than according to the depth of the purse of the patron: reasonably good work could be provided for those who could pay for it, but commonplace stuff was all that the less affluent could provide. Fifteenth-century sculpture in England was often respectable, but rarely fresh or inventive. The best is to be found no longer in building sculpture, but in the produc-

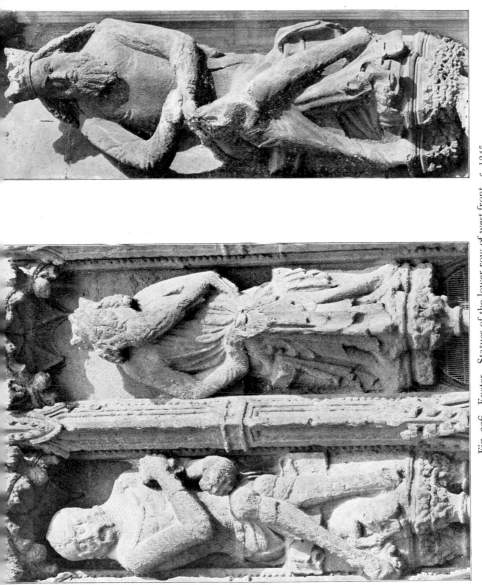

Fig. 326. Exeter. Statues of the lower row of west front. *c.* 1345.

tions of the furnishing trades, in tombs and screens and chantries. The most imaginative work was probably in the misericords of the stalls, where the wood-carvers were less bound by precedent and were able to give fuller play to their inventive skill.

(2) ARCHITECTURAL STATUES

The first effects of the changed conditions may be studied on the west front of Exeter Cathedral, which provides our greatest collection of fourteenth-century sculpture. It was begun by Bishop Grandisson (1327–69), and the lower stage must have been completed before the Plague years as the knight in Fig. 326 is wearing the short-fronted sur-coat, which was not worn after about 1345. The lower range of statues should therefore, strictly speaking, have been dealt with in the preceding chapter. The upper row is, however, of a rather different character, and, as a shield with the arms of Richard II is carved on it, it seems that the façade can only have been completed by Grandisson's suc-cessor, Bishop Brantyngham, somewhere about 1375 or 1380. There are 88 figures, including the angel brackets beneath the statues of the lower row. Of these three are modern substitutes and three or four have modern heads, but the rest are fairly genuine though sadly decayed, and in the absence of the protection originally given by the colouring the decay seems to be increasing more rapidly.

Though the work appears to have been spread over some thirty or forty years the original scheme planned by Grandisson must have been carried out, but the later sculpture of the upper tiers falls short of the earlier in some of its essential qualities. Decay of attributes makes the identification of individual figures difficult, but it is obvious that the old attempt to name the statues after kings of England was very wide of the mark. The central group of the upper tier was a Coronation of the Virgin, at present disguised by the substitution of a ridiculous figure of a king to replace the statue of Our Lady destroyed at the Reformation. On either side are ranged the Apostles

Fig. 327. Exeter. West front. The statues of the upper tier. "John", "James" and "Simon". *c.* 1380.

and Prophets. On the buttresses are the four Evangelists, and below them four ecclesiastics (three with poor new heads) who may be the Doctors of the Church. Below are a range of kings and warriors who must represent the royal line of Judah, figuring here as ancestors of the Virgin. The earlier figures in the lower tier are the most romantic and picturesque sculptures which have come down to us. They are seated in varied attitudes with legs crossed, some thoughtful, some conversing, and some ready to spring into action. The kings have long faces, are very hirsute and some of them are stroking their long beards. Draperies are usually drawn tight across the upper part of the body, and fall in overlapping folds over the knees. The liveliness of pose should be compared with that of the sword-drawing knight effigies described in the last chapter (see Fig. 296).

The Apostles (Fig. 327) and Prophets in the upper tier, which date from after the Black Death, are still picturesque, though they are not quite so romantic. They are short broad figures, clad in broad smooth draperies on which rich patterning could have been added in gold or colours, and, with one exception which is turned sideways, they stand squarely in their niches. The whole effect when new and resplendent with painting and gilding must have been extremely picturesque, even if lacking in the dignity of their thirteenth-century predecessors at Wells or Lincoln.[1]

The same sculptors who began the Exeter west front must have been employed on the reredos at Christchurch (Fig. 328), where the same cross-legged attitudes, long heads and beards and high cheek bones are identical in handling. Here the principal figures were of wood plated with silver, and have consequently disappeared, but the Beer stone figures remain, and as they are under cover they are sufficiently well preserved to enable us to form a better opinion of what the Exeter statues were like. The whole scheme was a great Tree of Jesse. Jesse lies at the base with the stem growing out of his side and winding

---

[1] For a complete description and illustrations see E. K. Prideaux, *The Figure Sculpture of the West Front of Exeter Cathedral Church.*

Fig. 328. Christchurch (Hants). Reredos of Beer stone.
"Jesse" and "Magi". *c.* 1350.

among the niches containing his descendants. On each side of him
are David and Solomon, and, above, the Adoration of the Magi.
A moment's comparison of the Exeter kings with the David, extending
even to the pearl ornament on the uprights dividing the niches, will
satisfy the inquirer as to a common authorship.

269

Fig. 329. British Museum. Ivory triptych. *c.* 1340.

We have not attempted as a rule to deal here with small portable objects like ivories, whose origin is difficult to prove,[1] but a triptych in the British Museum may be illustrated here as a work of the Exeter school, as it has the same long heads and an escutcheon and badge have been identified as those of Bishop Grandisson (Fig. 329).

The picturesque western style may also be recognised in the nine orders of angels of the central gable of the Wells west front, which were evidently added at a later date than the thirteenth-century work

[1] For the best account of ivory sculpture in England see Miss M. H. Longhurst's *English Ivories*, with beautifully reproduced illustrations.

270

Fig. 330. Wells Cathedral. Statues on the upper part of west front.

below them (Fig. 330). The Apostles above them are stiff and un-
gainly figures, designed for effect at a great distance, and we may
suppose these all placed in the earlier niches when the western towers
were raised, in 1386 and 1425, the Apostles belonging to the later
period. The angels appear to have been coloured a rosy red.

The statues of the Madonna which adorn the gateways of William of
Wykeham's College at Winchester, *c.* 1390 (Figs. 332, 333), are among
the finest productions of this period, that on the outer gateway being
fortunately well preserved. As is natural in hieratic statues of the kind
the traditional type of the Madonna has been retained, and apart from

Fig. 331. Thornton Abbey. Gateway. *c.* 1380.

Fig. 332. Winchester College. Virgin of the "Annunciation". *c.* 1390.

Fig. 333. Winchester College. The "Madonna". *c.* 1390.

the large crown and rather broad features and the flower sceptre, they might have been taken for work of fifty or sixty years earlier.

External sculpture at this date tends to become commonplace and designed for pictorial effect rather than close examination. The statues, for instance, on the gateway at Thornton Abbey (Fig. 331) are clumsy if looked at in detail, but they fit their position in the architectural scheme and the broad sweeping folds of their draperies would have lent themselves to colour decoration.

Niches were still prepared on the Perpendicular towers, which were not always filled subsequently with figures. At Beverley one ancient figure remains (Fig. 335), but the general impression we get of these statues is that they may be respectable but tend to become more and more uninspired shopwork and to reproduce stereotyped models without much fresh invention or imagination. A good idea of this type of work may be obtained from the row of playing-card kings inserted over the central west door at Lincoln in the latter part

Fig. 334. Lincoln. West front. Statues above doorway. *c.* 1380.

Fig. 335. Beverley. North side of north-west
tower. *c.* 1400.

Fig. 336. Lincoln. Gateway.
c. 1480.

18-2

Fig. 337. Winchester. Colossal
statue in crypt. *c.* 1400.

Fig. 338. Newark. Madonna on
south porch. *c.* 1450.

of the fourteenth century (Fig. 334), or in such statues as the Virgin Annunciate on the Stonebow Gateway at Lincoln (Fig. 336) or the Madonna of the south porch at Newark, *c.* 1450 (Fig. 338). A colossal statue now in the crypt at Winchester (Fig. 337), said to have come from the west front of the cathedral, probably represents St Swithin, and may be taken as the stock model of a bishop of the beginning of the fifteenth century.

(3) IMAGERS' SCULPTURE

The interest now shifts to the statues prepared for internal decoration of screen and altar. Many a great reredos was erected on the plan of that at Christchurch, the most notable being at Winchester, St Albans, New College Oxford, and Southwark. From all of these the images which crowded the niches have been removed, but certain fragments dug up here and there may have come from them. There are some splendid heads now in the Winchester Cathedral Library[1] (Figs. 339, 340) which may have come from some such position, and show a refinement coupled with dramatic power and mastery of technique that we hardly found in the purely architectural figures.

The organ screen at Canterbury has a row of six kings, rather above life size (Fig. 341), who probably represent kings of England and no longer the royal line of Judah. They carry orb and sceptre, and in one case a model of a church, and they wear robes capably rendered and falling in bold and deeply undercut folds at the side. The date does not seem to be recorded, but they are probably early fifteenth-century work. A later screen of similar type exists at York, where there are also a number of English kings. The style is remarkable, with bunched-out hair, and an extraordinary enforcement of line by deep undercutting (Fig. 342). It has been suggested that this has been derived from the art of glass painting, which was in great repute at York, and it is not unreasonable to conjecture that we have

---

[1] Some of these, together with others and a number of fragments formerly in the feretory, etc., have been recently collected in a kind of museum formed in the triforium of the transept.

Figs. 339, 340. Winchester. Heads in Cathedral Library.

here one of the productions of the Drawswerd shop mentioned in our introductory chapter (p. 18).

In the panelling at the end of the Divinity School at Oxford, and in the mouldings against the wonderful fan-vault there, niches are contrived which still retain a number of delicately wrought statuettes (Figs. 344, 350) dating from soon after 1450. Others are set in the pendant bosses, and show that the imagers could still produce work of considerable distinction.

But the chief collections of late Gothic imagery are at Westminster, and provide us with first-rate examples at an interval of sixty or seventy years. Henry V's chantry, according to Sir William Hope, was not completed till 1440 or 1450, though the king himself had projected some such erection in his will, and the actual tomb was set up soon after his death in 1422. The chantry was probably erected under the direction of John Thirsk, mason. It is built in the form of an **H** (Fig. 345) supported by two open-work towers joined by a cross-piece. The tomb was on the floor level, and above it was a

278

Fig. 341. Canterbury. Choir-screen. "Kings of England", about seven feet high. *c.* 1400.

Fig. 342. York Minster. Statue on choir-screen. "King Henry V." c. 1480.

Fig. 343. Westminster Abbey. Henry V's Chantry. "The Confessor." c. 1440.

Fig. 344. Oxford. Divinity School. Panel at end. *c.* 1452.

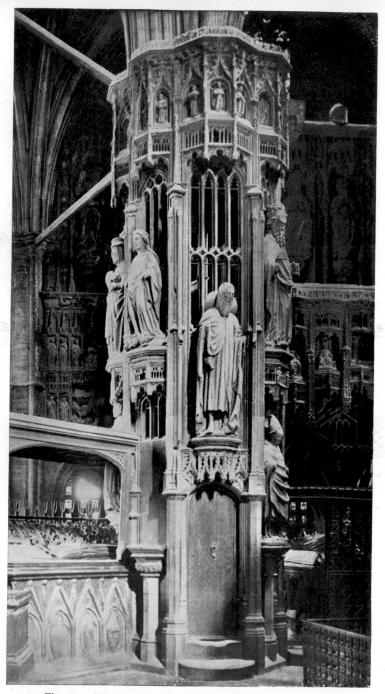

Fig. 345. Westminster. Pier of Henry V's Chantry. *c.* 1440.

Fig. 346. Westminster. Henry V's Chantry. "Coronation of the King."
c. 1440.

little chapel with an altar piece with an Annunciation, St Edward,
St Edmund, St George and St Denis, together with a vacant niche.[1]
On the staircase towers a number of statues are placed, including the
Confessor and the Pilgrim (to whom the king gave his ring, and who

[1] For fuller illustration of all these Westminster statues see the volume on the Abbey
published by the Royal Commission on Historical Monuments.

afterwards turned out to be St John), two kings, two bishops, a cardinal, a deacon and two or three other statues (Figs. 343, 347, 348). They are mostly fine and dignified figures, well proportioned and with draperies boldly wrought. In one or two of them the long fluttering hair and beard are marks of the dramatic ideals of the period, but they are not carried to such excess as in the York kings. The Confessor originally wore a metal crown, the holes for fixing which can be clearly seen. At the sides of the chantry the arches over the ambulatory are elaborately carved with the king's badges and with niches containing two representations of the coronation, probably not the two coronations as King of England and of France, as usually stated, but two incidents in the coronation service, the acclamation and the homage, as on one side the attendant nobles are bare-headed, and on the other they are wearing hats (Fig. 346).

Henry VII's Chapel was begun in 1502 and was almost complete in 1512, but although entirely built in the sixteenth century it contains no evidence of the Renaissance apart from Torrigiano's tomb in the centre. Robert Vertue, Robert Jenins and John Lebons were the King's master masons, but they were probably more concerned with the marvellous architectural structure than with the images that adorned it, and Lawrence Ymber, who made estimates for the images of the tomb, is a more likely candidate for the honour of having carved some of them.

The whole of the exterior stone-work has been renewed, and the statues there have all disappeared, but inside there are still about a hundred statues in fairly good preservation. All round the building at triforium level are a range of niches containing figures less than life size. Christ, the Virgin and Apostles are grouped at the east end, and all the most popular saints of the day are ranged to north and south. They are full of character and variety with a tendency to dramatic exaggeration in the large hats and billowy draperies. The St Anne teaching the infant Mary to read is one of the most pleasing

Fig. 347. Westminster. Henry V's
Chantry. "King."

Fig. 348. Westminster. Henry V's
Chantry. "Deacon."

Fig. 349. Westminster. Henry
VII's Chapel. Statue of
"St Anne". *c.* 1510.

Fig. 350. Oxford. Divinity
School.

of them (Fig. 349). In some the heads are too large, and several are actually wearing spectacles.

Larger statues are placed in elaborate niches supported by angel cornices in the chapels which radiate round the apse. These are also picturesque figures, though the proportions are more natural than those above. St Sebastian between the two archers who were to execute him form a dramatic group (Fig. 351) and the representation

286

Fig. 351. Westminster. Henry VII's Chapel. "St Sebastian"
and "Angel" cornice. c. 1510.

The Confessor.   St Peter.   St Edmund.

Fig. 352. Westminster. Henry VII's Chapel. c. 1510.

Fig. 353. Warwick.
Beauchamp Chapel.
c. 1450.

Fig. 354. Tong. c. 1520.

of the nude is not a bad attempt on the part of sculptors who were
seldom called upon for anything of the kind. The elaborately curled
locks of the Confessor and St Edmund, who stand on each side of
St Peter (Fig. 352), and the crumpled folds of their heavy draperies

are an attempt at realism, and throughout there is a freedom of pictorial representation a little outside the old medieval conventions, but at a time when Italian art of the Renaissance was at its height there is no sign of classicism.

If Tudor sovereigns set the example of building the most magnificent mausoleum ever erected in the country, their most powerful subjects followed their lead in the founding of gorgeous chapels to contain their own monuments. One of the finest of these is the Beauchamp Chapel at Warwick, built to contain the tomb of Richard Beauchamp, the famous Earl of Warwick. We shall deal with the actual tomb later, but part of the splendid stone decoration survives in the statuettes arranged in niches all round the east window. They represent saints (Fig. 353) and angels, and are certainly imagers' work. Much colour remains to give an idea of the sumptuous appearance of such a memorial chapel.

Finally, in the Golden Chapel at Tong, Salop, is the curious bust of Sir Arthur Vernon, priest, who died in 1517 (Fig. 354). He is represented as though preaching with a book before him, and his tomb with a brass showing him in academical robes is just below.

(4) Lesser Architectural Sculpture

The architectural sculpture of the fifteenth century need not detain us long. It follows the traditions of the fourteenth, but with a tendency to deteriorate into stereotyped forms and repetitions. Gargoyles still show a certain amount of imagination in the devils and monsters pressed into this service. They can be found all over the country on Perpendicular towers and the parapets which were so often reconstructed when bigger clerestory windows were added to older churches. Examples from Newark, *c.* 1450 (Fig. 355), and Croscombe, near Wells, must suffice here (Fig. 356).

Bosses in the high vault at Norwich carry on the Tewkesbury tradition. The nave vault was built by Bishop Lyhart after a fire in

Fig. 355. Newark. Gargoyle of chancel. *c.* 1450.

Fig. 356. Croscombe (Somerset). Gargoyles. South side. *c.* 1450.

19-2

Fig. 357. Norwich. Nave. "Massacre of Innocents." *c.* 1450.

1463. The 328 bosses illustrate the Bible story in both Old and New Testaments. A section is shown here with Herod and the Massacre of the Innocents (Fig. 357). Though effective at a distance the figures are crude puppets if examined closely, and the scenes seem copied from manuscript originals. The bosses nearer the eye in the north and west walks of the Norwich cloister are very inferior to the earlier carvings in the walks built in the previous century. Such versions as Herod's Feast, with Salome performing the licentious dance in the tumbling manner which had been assigned to her since the thirteenth century (Fig. 358), or a Nativity (Fig. 359) with its monotonous lines, are ineffective, shallow and confused in composition beside the earlier examples. In the Worcester cloister, *c.* 1390, there is a Jesse tree, and a curious Madonna holding the Child straight in front of her, and surrounded by the Four Beasts and angels (Fig. 360). The vault of the choir at Gloucester, *c.* 1370, has a regular choir of angels

Fig. 358. Norwich. Cloister.
"Herod's Feast." *c.* 1420.

Fig. 359. Norwich. North walk
of cloister. *c.* 1420.

playing musical instruments on its bosses (Fig. 361). Angels, in fact, become the stock motive of decoration, and appear everywhere as supporters of brackets, as bosses, filling spandrels as at Sall (Fig. 367), or forming cornices as at Southwark, Westminster (see Fig. 351) and Windsor (Fig. 362). They are no longer the great heavenly beings of the thirteenth century, weighing souls or expelling our first parents from Paradise, but have become little more than fairies whose functions are to hold up scrolls or shields of arms, and to minister to the glorification of human masters. Angels at King's College Chapel, Cambridge, holding up the royal arms have only the same function as the monsters (Fig. 363) and heraldic beasts (Fig. 364) which become an important item in the sculptural decoration of this period. Frequently, as in the Sall spandrel (Fig. 367), they are shown as feathered all over instead of wearing the usual alb; this was probably a remi-

293

Fig. 360. Worcester. Bosses of north walk of cloister.
c. 1390.

niscence of the feathered tights in which actors of such parts appeared
in the mystery plays, which were coming more and more into fashion.
A good example of the decorative use of heraldic devices combined
with little figures of saints in niches may be found in Prince Arthur's
chantry at Worcester dating from 1504 (Fig. 365).

Great angels with outspread wings were a feature of the famous
hammer-beam roofs of the eastern counties, and when glowing with
fresh colours must have produced a very splendid effect, though they

Fig. 361. Gloucester. Vault of choir. "Angel Musicians" above the high altar. *c.* 1350.

Fig. 362. Windsor. "Angel" cornice in St George's Chapel. *c.* 1500.

Fig. 363. King's College Chapel, Cambridge. (a) Heraldic dragon. c. 1510. (b) Heraldic angel. c. 1480.

Fig. 364. King's College Chapel. Internal heraldic sculpture.
c. 1510.

look rough and clumsy when detached from their positions. Statues of Apostles and others were also used by the wood-carvers to support the brackets as at March (Fig. 366), and the fluttering wings of the angel host spread all over the roof of the church caught the imagination of the people, and this scheme was repeated in many grand timber roofs, as at Wymondham, Cawston (Fig. 368) and many other places.

297

Fig. 365. Worcester. Prince Arthur's chantry.

(5) Fonts

It is time now to turn to the furniture sculpture which plays a more
important part as time goes on. Among the fittings necessary for
the larger parish churches, which in the fifteenth century were
ousting the monastic churches in popular favour, fonts were again
in demand. For some reason after the Norman fonts had ceased to
be made figure-sculpture was very seldom used, and during the
thirteenth and early fourteenth centuries arcading, mouldings, or
occasionally foliage were almost exclusively used for font decoration.
In the second half of the fourteenth century, however, figures were
again called into use for the purpose, and at Burford there is a tub-
font with a Crucifixion and saints under crocketed canopies carved
upon it (Fig. 369).

Fig. 366. March (Cambs). Roof of nave. c. 1450.

Fig. 367. Sall (Norfolk). West doorway.
c. 1475.

Fig. 368. Cawston. Nave
roof. c. 1475.

The most important developments in this line are to be found in
the eastern counties, where the wealth derived from the wool and
textile trade, of which these counties were the centre, encouraged
the building of splendid parish churches during the fifteenth century.
Two or three types are repeated again and again, and it is evident
that there were regular shops sending out stock patterns in all direc-
tions. One of these was no doubt situated in Norwich, whence
carriage of such bulky objects by water up the various estuaries was
not difficult, and another may have been at Ipswich. A full classification of these fonts depends mainly on shape and general design and
belongs to the study of ecclesiology generally rather than to one of
sculpture,[1] as the figure work is mere shop production and has little

[1] The reader may be referred to F. Bond's *Fonts and Font Covers* for a full treatment of
the subject. This contains over 400 photographs and drawings of all periods.

Fig. 369. Burford (Oxon). Figure-carved font.
c. 1350.

claim to distinction as sculpture. It will, therefore, only be necessary
here to illustrate a few typical examples to show their general position
in the story of our native art.

The font at Orford (Fig. 370) may be taken as a specimen of a
common type. The base is supported by clumsy lions alternating
with Wodehouses (or savage men). The bowl is supported by demi-
figures of angels with outspread wings, and is divided by buttresses

301

Fig. 370. Orford (Suffolk). "Evangelist" font.
c. 1400.

into oblong panels containing the Evangelistic symbols and sacred figures such as the Trinity.

Another type occurs in Norwich All Saints' (Fig. 371), and has almost a duplicate in St James's Church in the same city. Here the shaft is divided into niches containing stiff figures by mouldings

Fig. 372. East Dereham (Norfolk). "Seven Sacraments" font. c. 1470.

Fig. 371. Norwich. All Saints' Church. Apostle font. c. 1420.

which are continued upwards to form branches of foliage to cover the swelling part beneath the bowl. The square compartments of the latter are occupied by pairs of saints.

Another series fills the panels with little reliefs of the Seven Sacraments with the eighth panel occupied by a Baptism of Christ, a Crucifixion, an Assumption or some such scene. A good example may be found at East Dereham (Fig. 372), on which niches are contrived on the stem as well as the lions and other figures on the base. In this, too, elaborate lierne vaulting is given to the heads of the niches and the bowl panels, and these later fonts are often raised on stepped platforms with panelled sides, which gives a dignified effect. The actual figure work becomes more perfunctory and mechanical as time goes on, and the interest is centred more on the subjects of the reliefs than on the execution. No doubt when new and gay with colour they were more effective than they are now in the mutilated condition so many of them are in, making the details difficult to identify.

(6) WOOD-SCULPTURE

In the fifteenth century the carpenter's art reached a new level of attainment in the splendid hammer-beam roofs of East Anglia, in the screens of Norfolk, Suffolk and Devon, and in the stalls of cathedrals and collegiate churches all over England. This is not the place to describe the elaborate tabernacles and canopies, but the art of the figure carver was called in to complete and give life to the rest.

The great wooden roods, flanked by statues of St Mary and St John on the beams which spanned the chancel of nearly every church, and the figures which must have decked many an altar have all been ruthlessly swept away by iconoclastic reformers, and only an odd fragment here and there remains to give any idea of what they were like.[1]

[1] A series of statuettes at South Kensington, a Madonna at York, a repainted statue of a fourteenth-century queen in the Library of Queen's College, Oxford, and two figures forming an Annunciation in the Hall of the Vicar's Choral at Wells, a group of St Anne the Virgin and Child at South Kensington, and a much worn Pietà at Battlefield may be cited as among the most important survivals of wooden images.

Fig. 373. Winchester. Stalls. *c.* 1300.

Stalls in England are remarkable for their rich and elaborate canopies, but these are not usually fitted with statuettes, though late examples occur at Windsor. The large dorsal reliefs common on the Continent are conspicuous by their absence, though small figures occur among the foliage in the earliest of our fine stalls at Winchester (Fig. 373). The ends of benches are not infrequently richly decorated, as at Ripon and Chester. Fine carved bench-ends also occur in smaller churches and we may take as examples the St Michael at Haverford-west (Fig. 374) and the St Andrew at St Ives, Cornwall (Fig. 375).

Fig. 374. Haverfordwest
(Pembroke). *c.* 1490.

Fig. 375. St Ives (Cornwall).
c. 1520.

Fig. 376. Boston (Lincs). Arm of stall.
c. 1400.

In these Cornish churches the Gothic tradition of the carving of benches lingered on well into the sixteenth century, and at Mullion we see Renaissance putti playing with wine casks in the midst of Gothic tracery and next door to reliefs of the Instruments of the Passion.

Stall arms frequently have animals crawling over them, as at Boston (Fig. 376), and bench-ends are usually carried up to form a foliated finial usually called a poppy-head.[1] Most of these are merely foliage, but figures are sometimes introduced as in the elaborate specimens we give from King's Lynn (Fig. 377), Walpole St Peter (Fig. 378), and Ludlow (Fig. 379). Sometimes little figures are perched on the arm beside them, as at Fressingfield (Fig. 382), and sometimes the whole poppy-head is replaced by a figure, as in the interesting set of the Seven Deadly Sins at Blythburgh (Fig. 381).

It is in the eastern counties that the carving of bench-ends reaches its highest perfection. Until the fifteenth century provision of seating

---

[1] Supposed to be derived from "puppis", a poop. Some purists prefer to use an old form "popey".

Fig. 377. King's Lynn. St Nicholas.
"Poppy-head." *c.* 1415.

Fig. 378. Walpole St Peter (Norfolk).
"Poppy-head." *c.* 1450.

accommodation for the congregation was very scanty and elaborate
decoration was reserved for the stalls of the clergy in cathedral or
collegiate churches. When, however, the increase of trade and manu-
facture brought wealth to the middle classes of East Anglia it became
the fashion to fit out the naves of many of the fine new parish churches
with a complete set of benches, and these were often enriched with
carving and poppy-heads. Perhaps the finest are the late fifteenth-
century examples at Wiggenhall St Mary the Virgin, where the

Fig. 379. Ludlow. "Poppy-head."
c. 1440.

Fig. 380. Wiggenhall St Mary.
Bench-end. c. 1500.

bench-ends have a figure of a prophet or saint in a niche and lively
little figures are seated on each side of the poppy-head (Fig. 380).
There is a rather earlier set with standing figures and less elaboration

309

Fig. 381. Blythburgh. "Sloth". c. 1470.   Fig. 382. Fressingfield. c. 1490.

of detail on the other side of the church, and another interesting set
at Wiggenhall St German, where an angel is pointing to the usurer,
drunkard, etc., descending into the mouth of Hell. Others at
Fressingfield, mentioned above, Dennington and St Nicholas, King's
Lynn, are among the richest examples.

In Devonshire and the west country benches are usually square-
topped, and there is a tendency to cover the whole of the bench-end
with tracery or foliage patterns.[1]

[1] For illustrations of bench-ends and woodwork generally see Howard and Crossley's
magnificently illustrated book on *English Church Woodwork*.

Fig. 383. Westminster. Henry VII's Chapel. "The Scolding Wife."
c. 1520.

It is, however, in the *misericords*, as the seats made to turn up and form a bracket to give support during the long services were called, that the wood-carver found fullest opportunity for his art. There are more than two thousand of these little carvings in parish churches as well as cathedrals, and as they seem to have been less subject to clerical censorship and dictation than the more essentially religious sculptures they form a mine of inexhaustible wealth for the researchers after medieval iconography. They display a liveliness of imagination, a sense of humour and power of composition that seems to have died out in the more formal productions of the stone-masons and imagers of the fifteenth century.

The subjects represented cover the whole field of medieval life and thought. From simple foliage and grotesques they pass on to heraldry and scenes from everyday life. We see the carver of the misericord himself at work (Fig. 7), the huntsman, the farmer, the tournament (Fig. 384). The schoolmaster with birch rod brandished holds his unfortunate pupil across his knees (Fig. 3), the scolding wife belabours her spouse with her distaff (Fig. 383), the boatmen put to sea and a passenger is sea-sick (Fig. 386), or undergraduates listen to a lecture at Oxford (Fig. 387). Agriculture is well represented in most of the big series, as in the vintage at Gloucester (Fig. 388), and the works

311

Fig. 384. Worcester. Misericord. "Tournament." *c.* 1400.
Fig. 385. Worcester. Misericord. "Judgment of Solomon." *c.* 1400.

Fig. 386. St David's. *c.* 1470.
Fig. 387. Oxford, New College. *c.* 1480.

of the various months, as at Worcester, etc. Satire even on the clergy
is frequent, and we see the fox preaching to the geese (Fig. 389),
or an ass or an ape chanting the responses. Popular romances such as
that of Reynard the Fox, or Alexander's flight to the ends of the earth

313

Fig. 388. Gloucester. "The Vintage."
c. 1360.

supported by griffins (Fig. 390), or combats between lions and dragons occur again and again. Perhaps the most fruitful source of all was the Bestiary, a kind of medieval natural history book which described all kinds of beasts fabulous or otherwise, embellished with all sorts of old wives' tales, and ending up with a far-fetched moral. Thus the huntsman carrying off the young of the tiger at Chester (Fig. 2) is seen strewing mirrors in the way, as described on p. 8. Fabulous creatures like the mermaid (Fig. 391) are grouped with real beasts like the tiger, lion, elephant or whale, but the stories about them are hardly less incredible than those about the real creatures.

Bible stories, too, are frequent, the Old Testament being more common than the New. Samson carrying off the gates of Gaza (Fig. 392) and Jonah and the Whale (Fig. 393) at Ripon at the end of the fifteenth century are carved with as much spirit and verve as earlier work at Lincoln or Gloucester. The Crucifixion and such serious subjects do not occur, but at Sherborne there is a formidable Last Judgment with Christ seated on the rainbow and the dead rising from their tombs (Fig. 394).

314

Fig. 389. Beverley Minster. "The Fox preaching to the geese."
c. 1520.

Fig. 390. Wells. "Alexander's flight."
c. 1330.

The saints are surprisingly rare. There are a few examples of the
Evangelists, as at Worcester, St Martin and St Giles appear at Ely,
and at Norwich and some other places there is a St George (Fig. 395),

Fig. 391. Ludlow. "Mermaid." *c.* 1440.

Fig. 392. Ripon Minster. "Samson and the gates of Gaza."
c. 1500.

though in the latter case it is not always easy to say whether St George is definitely indicated or whether we merely have a combat between a warrior and dragon.

In shape the English misericords follow a line of their own. On the Continent sculpture is always confined to the central support,

Fig. 393. Ripon Minster. "Jonah and the Whale." *c.* 1500.

Fig. 394. Sherborne. "The Last Judgment." *c.* 1440.

but in England this is usually balanced by two supporters or "ears". In the earliest thirteenth-century examples these are sometimes omitted, as in the beautiful example we give from Christchurch (Fig. 396), or they are comparatively small and composed merely of a spray of foliage or dragon head, as at Exeter (Fig. 397). Later they become larger, though a spreading leaf or grinning face is often

317

Fig. 395. Norwich. "St George and Dragon." *c.* 1400.

Fig. 396. Christchurch (Hants). *c.* 1220.

used, and grotesques or animal subjects become common. Sometimes subjects subsidiary to the main theme are employed, like the
extra pupils of the schoolmaster at Norwich (Fig. 3) or the hens
listening to the preaching fox at Boston (Fig. 398), or else they form
part of the group like the tigers at Chester (Fig. 2). Sometimes the

Fig. 397. Exeter. *c.* 1260.

Fig. 398. Boston. "Fox and hens." *c.* 1400.

ears are almost as important as the main bracket, as at Sherborne (Fig. 394), or in the elaborate Judgment of Solomon at Worcester (Fig. 385); more rarely the whole flat part of the seat is thrown into one design by cusping, as at Gloucester (Fig. 388).

It is remarkable what variety of handling is to be found in the different sets, and it looks as though each great cathedral developed its own local types. The earliest examples, like those at Exeter (Fig. 397), are based on stone-mason's technique, and are not far removed from the little figures on the Wells capitals, but practice soon worked

319

out a more distinctive wood technique. The very distinct mannerisms of Worcester or the special designs at Gloucester distinguish them from an entirely different style at Lincoln, Ely, or Carlisle.[1]

(7) BRONZE AND ALABASTER, ALTAR AND TOMB, 1360–1540

So far we have examined the sculpture of screen and chantry, and it remains to review that of the altars or tombs which were the centre of these erections. The art of the imagers was transformed after the Black Death not only by the new social conditions and consequent commercial development of the trade, but also by the introduction of a fresh and beautiful material. The Derbyshire alabaster is a form of gypsum, and differs from continental or oriental alabaster, and it is found near Tutbury and Chellaston, a few miles south of Derby. It does not stand exposure to the weather, but is easy to work, suitable for fine detail and takes colour well. Its earliest use is in one of the inner orders of the rich late Norman doorway of Tutbury Priory (Fig. 426). There was a royal castle at Tutbury, largely rebuilt by John of Gaunt, and it is not unlikely that as Purbeck marble came into favour owing to royal patronage, the same may have been the case with alabaster. There is a record[2] that John of Gaunt gave instructions to his agent at Tutbury to send six cartloads of alabaster for the tomb of his wife in 1374, and his own monument in old St Paul's appears to have been in this material. There seems good reason, therefore, to suppose that London, having no stone of its own, imported alabaster along with other materials for the use of its school of imagers.

[1] For a more complete treatment of the subject the reader must be referred to F. Bond's *Misericords*, containing numerous photographs. Miss E. Philipson's *Choir Stalls and their Carvings* is also a useful collection, though the drawings are not so good as photographs in more modern books.

[2] P. B. Chatwin, "Monumental Effigies in Warwickshire" (*Birmingham Arch. Soc. Trans.* 1921).

(a) Bronze

Before discussing the output of the alabaster-men, it will be best to describe the later bronze tombs erected for royal or very distinguished persons, as they to some extent served as a model for all the others to follow.

The first of these to be made after Henry III and Queen Eleanor was that of the Black Prince, d. 1376, at Canterbury (Fig. 399). In his will he directed that "an image shall be placed in memory of us all armed in steel for battle", and the sculptor has taken the utmost pains to render every detail of the armour, which is typical of the last quarter of the fourteenth century, when plate was beginning to replace mail on arms and legs. The prince wears the pointed bascinet, from which the camail depends, and there is a coronet round it. The jupon, which was probably still of leather, worn over mail, has the royal arms in bold relief. The legs are straight, as the cross-legged attitude would no longer be comfortable in steel plate, and the hands are clasped in prayer. Little of the face is exposed, and we can hardly call this a portrait, nothing more than a general typical warrior being intended. The bronze technique has been thoroughly mastered, but the stiff pose necessitated by the growing elaboration of the armour prevents the variety of action or the more romantic attitudes of the previous generation.

Edward III's own effigy is rather severe in its straight lines and balanced pose with a sceptre in each hand to represent England and France. The individual features and long beard give this figure a better claim to be a portrait than anything we have yet seen (Fig. 400). No account of the making of this tomb has been preserved, but we know that John Orchard, "latoner", was in the king's employ at this time and supplied railings and six angels for Queen Philippa's[1] tomb, and he was very likely responsible

[1] Her effigy is of white marble, and was made by a foreign artist, Hawkin Liège of France (Fig. 403).

G   321   21

Fig. 399. Canterbury. Bronze effigy of Black Prince. d. 1376.

Fig. 400. Westminster. Confessor's Chapel. Bronze effigy of Edward III. d. 1377.

Fig. 401. Westminster. Bronze
weeper from Edward III's
tomb.

Fig. 402. Westminster. Bronze
weeper from Edward III's
tomb.

for the bronze work of Edward III's tomb. The tomb-chest is
of Purbeck marble, and on it stand as weepers six little bronze
figures of his family (Figs. 401, 402). These are excellent specimens of the fashionable costume of the time, the tight bodice with
large buttons and stiff framed head-dress of the princess being most
characteristic.

Fig. 403 Westminster. Confessor's Chapel. Marble effigy of Queen Philippa. *c.* 1370.

Fig. 404. Westminster. Confessor's Chapel. Bronze effigies of Richard II and Queen. *c.* 1395.

Fig. 405. Warwick. Bronze head of "Richard Beauchamp".
c. 1454.

The effigies of Richard II and his Queen Anne were made in 1395 after the death of the queen (Fig. 404). In that year a contract was signed with Nicholas Broker and Godfrey Prest, citizens and coppersmiths of London, for two gilt images crowned and clasping their right hands. Details of all accessories were set out and instructions given for engraving the table on which they were placed. All was to be performed in two years according to a "patron" which Nicholas and Godfrey had shown the king, and they were to receive £400. Precious stones were set down the middle of the queen's bodice. The arms were cast separately and have been lost. As the king was still alive and taking an interest in the work there was probably some attempt at portraiture. If the work as ideal sculpture does not compare with Torel's figures of a hundred years earlier, these effigies at

325

Fig. 406. Warwick. Richard Beauchamp's monument.
c. 1454.

least were splendidly finished with elaborate accessories and presented a sumptuous appearance.

Henry V's effigy was of oak plated with silver, but only the battered
core of wood remains. One other magnificent bronze, however, survives on the tomb of Richard Beauchamp, Earl of Warwick, and here
again the contract has been preserved, as stated in our introductory
chapter (see p. 16). William Austen's figure (Fig. 405), in spite of
its peculiar visage, can hardly have been a portrait as it was made

326

"St James." "St George."

Figs. 407, 408. Henry VII's tomb. Bronze figures in screen. _c._ 1510.

in 1454, and the famous earl died in 1439. Austen undertook to make the "image of a man armed according to patterns", and he evidently took the greatest pains to represent the splendid Milanese armour of the earl in every detail. It is finished on the back as carefully as on the front, and the whole execution is masterly, even down to the veins on the hands. The tomb is of Purbeck marble, and in the niches are placed little figures of angels and weepers alternately. The weepers are clad in heavy mourning cloaks (Fig. 406), following the fashion set by the magnificent tombs of the Dukes of Burgundy at Dijon by the school of Claus Sluter,[1] and are masterpieces of their kind.

Henry VII's effigy and that of the Lady Margaret at Westminster were made by the Italian Torrigiano, but the superb grate enclosing the tomb is English work, and may with some probability be attributed to Laurence Ymber, who competed with Drawswerd of York for the original design which was never carried out. On the grate are several small bronze statuettes of considerable power and beauty. We illustrate two of them representing St James and St George (Figs. 407, 408) to show that native craftsmen were able to make figures fit to stand beside the masterpieces of the countryman and contemporary of Michelangelo.

The brasses, or flat incised plates of laton, which were such a popular form of memorial in our churches, are more drawings than sculpture and cannot be described here. They are useful for comparison and for settling points of costume and date, but for these the reader must be referred to the excellent monographs which deal with the subject.[2]

(b) Alabaster

Alabaster[3] seems to have come into general use during the second quarter of the fourteenth century, and after the Black Death its use increased rapidly until it set the fashion for all the other trades in

---

[1] See the author's *Medieval Sculpture in France*, Figs. 421, 422, 423.

[2] The most convenient is probably H. W. Macklin's *Brasses of England*, 1907. The Victoria and Albert Museum *List of Rubbings of Brasses* contains a very valuable series of illustrations from the rubbings.

[3] A very valuable paper "On the Early Working of Alabaster in England" was published by W. H. St John Hope, in the *Archaeological Journal*, 1904. Much of this was reprinted together with an article on "The Sculpture of Alabaster Tables" by E. S. Prior in the *Illustrated Catalogue of the Exhibition of English Medieval Alabaster Work* held at Burlington House, 1910.

religious and monumental sculpture. In the fifteenth century its reputation was so great that there is evidence of a considerable export trade to various parts of the Continent. For instance, Queen Joan, after her marriage to Henry IV, ordered an alabaster tomb for her first husband, John, Duke of Brittany (d. 1399), to be erected at Nantes. This was made by Thomas Colyn, Thomas Holewell and Thomas Poppehowe, and completed in 1408. A drawing of it exists, made before its destruction at the Revolution. In 1382 the king gave orders to the Customs officials at Southampton to allow the Pope's representative Cosmato Gentilis to export three images of alabaster, of the Virgin, St Peter and St Paul and a small one of the Trinity. Three small statues were discovered not long ago beneath the floor of the church at Flawford, and are now in the Nottingham Museum. The two finest of them, a Madonna, some 28 inches high (Fig. 409), and a St Peter in the garb of a medieval pope, a few inches higher (Fig. 410), still retain much of the elegance of early fourteenth-century style and have not developed the mannerisms of fifteenth-century commercial production. Later figures were mostly made in connection with the retables, of which they formed part, and display coarser handling and mass-production mannerisms. An enormous number of little reliefs about 15 inches high by about 11 inches broad, together with a number of larger panels, are scattered all over Europe in churches and museums, and until recently their origin was not realised. They are found as far away as Iceland and Italy, and beside those exported complete before the Reformation there is no doubt that a great number were sold abroad when they were turned out of our own churches by the reformers.[1] These were grouped in wooden frames to form reredoses or retables. None of these remain in England in their original positions, but a few complete specimens in their original settings survive in France,

[1] Sir William St John Hope found a letter from France in 1550 complaining that three or four ships laden with images had arrived and that the contents had been sold in Paris, Rouen and other places.

Fig. 409. Nottingham Museum.
"Madonna" from Flawford.

Fig. 410. Nottingham Museum.
"St Peter" from Flawford.

Fig. 411. South Kensington. Alabaster retable.

Fig. 412. Yssac-la-Tourette (Puy de Dome). "John Baptist" retable. *c.* 1450.

Germany, Italy and elsewhere, and the South Kensington Museum has acquired a complete specimen (Fig. 411), which preserves much of its colouring as well as the wooden frame, and helps to give a notion of the rich and gorgeous effect attained. Many of these panels, or tables as they were called, are crude in execution, and the harsh cutting and shop mannerisms are not attractive on close inspection, but when looked at from a distance, as they were intended to be, the rich and mellow colouring, the gilded hinges and Gothic lettering of the inscriptions between the tables produce a very beautiful impression, and the hard lines serve to bring out the subject-matter in a way which finer sculpture would have failed to attain. We illustrate two examples from France to show how these retables were made up. There were usually five or seven tables, the middle one being taller than the rest, and a single figure was often placed at the ends (Figs. 412, 413). Sometimes more elaborate erections were made with two tiers, and a number of small single figures between them. These are all late examples, but there is a record of very large sums being paid to Peter "maceon" of Nottingham for a large retable to be placed in the chapel of St George at Windsor, *c.* 1370, and in

Fig. 413. Compiègne Museum. Alabaster retable. *c.* 1480. The names of the
scenes are to be read in the original inscriptions.

1372 John Lord Nevill of Raby ordered a magnificent reredos of
alabaster for Durham Cathedral.

For these retables the panels were grouped in sets of suitable
subjects. Thus the Annunciation, Nativity, Magi, Circumcision,
Coronation of the Virgin with a tall central panel of the Assumption
would make a Virgin set, or a central panel of the Crucifixion would
have the various Passion scenes, the Betrayal, Flagellation, Entombment and Resurrection, grouped round it. These are the commonest,

333

Fig. 414. Long Melford (Suffolk). The "Adoration of the Magi".
Alabaster slab. *c.* 1350.

but panels devoted to the Baptist and other saints, a number of
martyrdom scenes and many other interesting subjects appear, though
the exact grouping is a matter of conjecture as the examples in
England have mostly been dug up one by one from beneath the floors
of churches or picked up separately by collectors all over Europe.[1]

The earliest tables may not always have been framed up to form
retables as they are finished off smoothly with a kind of edging all
round, as if for individual exhibition. Thus there is a long wide
panel in Long Melford Church representing the Magi, which would
not have fitted into the scheme of any complete reredos which has
survived (Fig. 414). Some broken slabs from Kettlebaston in the
British Museum are of exceptionally refined handling with the

---

[1] Several papers by Dr Hilburgh and Dr Nelson have been published in *Archaeologia*,
the *Archaeological Journal* and the journals of other antiquarian societies on these tables
and give examples of unusual subjects.

Fig. 415. British Museum. From Kettlebaston.
The "Coronation". *c.* 1350.

graceful overlapping draperies of the middle of the fourteenth century. One of these has the Coronation of the Virgin (Fig. 415)
treated in a novel way: she kneels to receive the crown instead of
being placed on a throne beside her Son, as in the thirteenth century,
and this contrasts also with a later fifteenth-century version where
she sits in front in the middle and is crowned by the three persons
of the Trinity.

Another group of panels may be separated as being fairly early,
as the costume of the figures and camail and jupon worn by the
soldiers point to a date in the fourteenth century. These are distinguished by having an embattled canopy worked in the same piece
as the rest of the slab, as shown in a Coronation of the old type and
a Resurrection at Ripon (Fig. 416). In the latter Christ steps from
the tomb with arm outstretched, whereas in the late versions his

335

Fig. 416. Ripon. Statuette and tables in vestry. "Coronation"
and "Resurrection". *c.* 1400.

arm is bent and held close to the shoulder. An Annunciation now
at Beauvais (Fig. 417) has the embattled canopy and the angel is
advancing quietly from the right instead of from the left, as usual.
The quiet dignity and delicate drapery mark this as retaining fourteenth-century style. The later treatment of this subject is more
dramatic. The angel kneels and holds out a scroll, while the Virgin
starts back with a gesture of surprise: between the two is a lily pot,
and a bust of God the Father appears at the top with a dove descending
from his mouth (Fig. 418). In the example we show[1] there is a
gabled canopy which serves to introduce the later fashion of making

[1] As, however, this panel is rather small it is possible it came from a tomb and not
a retable.

336

Fig. 417. Beauvais Museum. "Annunciation."
c. 1400.

a kind of cresting in the shape of a row of little traceried windows in a separate block to be fixed above the tables, as shown in the complete sets at South Kensington (Fig. 411) and elsewhere.

These later fifteenth-century tables are not finished off so carefully at the edges, and the vast majority of our surviving specimens have

Fig. 418. British Museum. "Annunciation."
c. 1450.

Fig. 419. Wells. "Annunciation"
on tomb-chest. c. 1440.

lost the cresting. They show an increasing tendency to coarser
handling and mannerisms as time goes on, though some of the uglier
features, like the bulging eyeballs, would have been modified when
the eyelids and lashes had been filled in with colour. The armour of
soldiers and executioners is of a later type and a kind of sallet
replaces the bascinet, but as these are usually only men at arms
exact dating is not so easy as in the case of the effigies of the
knights whose armour enables them to be dated very closely. In the

Fig. 421. Alabaster table. "St Edmund."
c. 1480.

Fig. 420. Alabaster table. Martyrdom of St Catherine.
c. 1480.

Fig. 422. The statuettes of an alabaster retable. *c.* 1450.

martyrdom scenes the executioners are given hideous faces, which seem
sometimes to have been painted black, and the onlookers wear large
hats (Fig. 420). In the St Edmund table (Fig. 421) the traceried
cresting has been preserved and is well seen.

In the latest examples the scenes become crowded and workmanship careless; exaggerations of anatomical details and affected attitudes show the last degradation to which the shop-carvers came
(Fig. 423). Certain tables with a large head of John the Baptist in

340

Fig. 423. Ashmolean Museum. "Crucifixion."
c. 1490.

Figs. 424, 425. "St John's Heads."
c. 1500.

a charger, a Resurrection below and saints on either side, seem to have been made for private worship, and were hawked about the country (Figs. 424, 425). In 1491 Nicholas Hill, an image-maker, brought an action against his salesman for the value of 58 heads of St John the Baptist, which shows the wholesale nature of the trade. The three small statuettes in Fig. 422 are excellent specimens of the small figures ranged between the tables in the reredoses.

The chief centre of the alabaster trade was in Nottingham and round the quarries, though at first it seems likely that the alabaster was sent to London to be carved. The great Durham altar-piece was to be sent in boxes from London. Alabaster workers, or "alablaster-men", as they are sometimes called, have left records at York, Lincoln, and later at Burton, and probably also existed at such important centres as Bristol and Norwich. It is, however, purely a matter of conjecture to try to assign definite types of panels to any special centre. Our only fixed point is the tomb at Lowick, where the contract with Chellaston workers has been preserved, but this has no special feature in common with the retables.

Besides the retables the alabaster shops were kept busy in providing the *tombs* which survive in great numbers, and which set the fashion for such monuments for nearly 200 years. Two wall-tombs exist at Bakewell and Youlgreave. The first (Fig. 427) is a monument to Sir Godfrey Foljambe, d. 1376, and he and his lady are shown as half figures looking out from beneath an ogee canopy, as from a window, and the top of the slab is embattled like the earlier tables. The Youlgreave slab is much later and commemorates Robert Gylbert, d. 1492, who kneels with his wife on each side of the Madonna, while his numerous sons and daughters fill the sides of the panel (Fig. 428).

These, however, are exceptions. The usual form of tomb consisted of a tomb-chest surmounted by the effigy of the deceased laid flat on his back with his head resting on cushions, or on a tilting helm

Fig. 426. Tutbury. First use of alabaster. *c.* 1160.
Fig. 427. Bakewell. Monument of Sir G. Foljambe. d. 1376.
Fig. 428. Youlgreave. Monument of Robert Gylbert. d. 1492.

Fig. 429. Dodford. End of tomb-chest. *c.* 1450.

if a knight, and his feet against a lion or other beast. Little angels sometimes sit beside the head, as on the earlier Westminster tombs, and pet dogs often take the place of lions at a lady's feet, and sometimes play with the hem of her skirts. There is little variety in pose, and we miss the more romantic handling of the stone and wood effigies of *c.* 1300, but this is to some extent made up for by the changes in costume and armour, which are very carefully studied, and the effigies give us a most interesting series illustrating the changes of fashion and accoutrements.

The tomb-chest was either set against a wall (Fig. 430), usually under an ogee canopy, or was standing free in the shape of what is called a table tomb. This might not always be of alabaster, any more than the canopies occasionally erected over it, and when alabaster was used the sides were sometimes panelled, but more frequently decorated with niches or later divided up by miniature buttresses

344

Fig. 430. Abergavenny. Wall tomb. *c.* 1510.
Fig. 431. Norbury. Table tomb. *c.* 1480.

Fig. 432. Abergavenny. End of tomb. *c.* 1450.

with crocketed canopies joining them, and in these niches were placed rows of "weepers", as they are called. These might be relatives, like the bronze sons and daughters of Edward III at Westminster, or they might be saints, or angels carrying shields blazoned with the family arms (Fig. 429). Sometimes religious scenes like those on the tables were introduced as on a tomb of an ecclesiastic at Wells (Fig. 419), where an Annunciation might have come straight from the same workshops as the retables. A later Annunciation with cresting very like that given to some of the later tables may be found on a tomb at Abergavenny (Fig. 432) and shows that the production of reredos and tomb was going on side by side in the same workshops. In the splendid tomb of the Earl at Arundel the weepers are the Canons of the College he had founded (Fig. 433). The tomb of Prince John of Eltham, son of Edward II, who died in 1334, has lost its superb canopy, but is remarkable as one of the first of

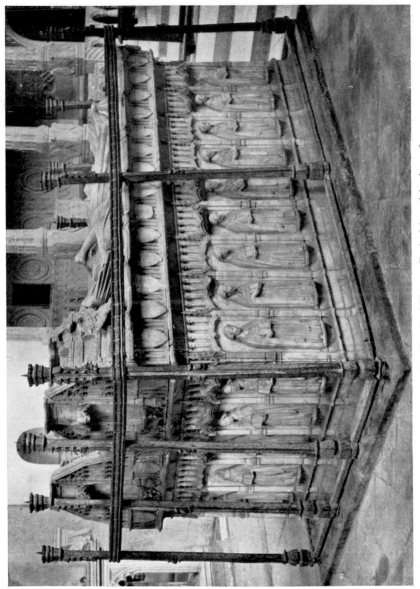

Fig. 433. Arundel. Tomb of Thomas Earl of Arundel. d. 1416.

Fig. 434. Warwick. Alabaster weepers of Earl and Countess of Warwick.
c. 1370.

the alabaster tombs. The weepers are cut out of alabaster, and the background pierced and backed up with a dark stone, this mixture of materials suggesting that it is a London work. The little weepers, who are mostly kings and queens, are lively and charming, though they lack the dignity of the earlier stone weepers on Crouchback's tomb. There are exaggerations of hands and other features to give emphasis, and they are full of life (see Fig. 275).

Alabaster weepers do not become common until after about 1370. Those on the tomb of Thomas Beauchamp, Earl of Warwick, who died in 1371, are excellent examples of the costumes of the period (Fig. 434). The short jerkin of the men, tight bodices and long cloaks of the women, produce rather a jaunty effect, though the framed or reticulated head-dresses of the ladies sometimes make them look somewhat grim. In the North the housings are sometimes omitted

348

Fig. 435. Swine. Alabaster tomb. *c.* 1420.
Fig. 436. Harewood. Tomb of Sir W. Gascoigne. *c.* 1420.

Fig. 437. Lowick.

Fig. 438. Merevale.

Fig. 439. Bottesford.

Fig. 440. Ashbourne.

Angel-weepers.

altogether, and angels holding shields, as at Swine and Harewood (Figs. 435, 436), kneeling in pairs on little footstools, are carved upon plain flat slabs. At Merevale they have a plain background (Fig. 438), and at Bottesford they occupy oblong framed panels (Fig. 439), but at Lowick the contract stipulated for "tabernacles", and we accordingly find the angels placed between little buttresses with a low ogee canopy over them (Fig. 437). They usually wear albs and a flat cap with the hair brushed up on each side of it, and the primary wing feathers are carved with tips turned up, the smaller feathers being left for insertion by the painters. The later angels usually wear low mitres or fillets with a cross set in the apex. In the second quarter of the fifteenth century a more formal system of panelling

Fig. 441. Ewelme (Oxon). Tomb of the Duchess of Suffolk. d. 1473.

351

on the lines of Perpendicular window tracery makes its appearance, as at Ashbourne (Fig. 440), and in the third quarter the usual arrangement was that with a loftier ogee canopy richly crocketed between the little buttresses, as at Norbury (Fig. 431). These later tomb-chests are often very elaborate; one favourite design was to have two little canopies over each figure with a pinnacle between them cut off above the heads and not carried down, as at Ewelme (Fig. 441). Here the shield-bearing angels, like the big wooden roof angels, are alternately clad in albs and in feathered tights.

In the latest tombs the weepers are often grouped in twos and threes, sometimes standing hand in hand, as at Ashover (Fig. 442), or else pose in mimic attitudes of grief, as at Kinlet (Fig. 443). In this last tomb, that of Sir John Blount, d. 1531, the first signs of Renaissance influence begin to appear. The scrolls forming the canopies are decidedly Flemish in type, but the figures themselves are still purely Gothic, though possibly rendered with slightly more delicacy than some of the later fifteenth-century figures.

In a late wall tomb at Abergavenny (Fig. 430) the weepers appear to be seated, and in the recess under the enclosing canopy an Annunciation slab, of the type made for the retables, is set with kneeling knights and ladies on each side, whose costume and armour is so exactly like that of the main effigy that these seem to be in their right position.

In some of the latest monuments the elaboration of the canopies is carried to an extreme and imitation vaulting is placed underneath them, while twisted shafts at the corners are heralds of the Renaissance. It is a curious fact that in one of the last pre-Reformation tombs, that of Sir Richard Knightley at Fawsley, the alabaster weepers are cut out and set against a black background, very much as those of John of Eltham had been placed at the first introduction of alabaster for tomb making.

Fig. 442. Ashover. Alabaster weepers. *c.* 1518.
Fig. 443. Kinlet. Alabaster weepers. *c.* 1531.

Effigy Types

Turning to the *effigies* themselves, it is impossible to give more than a few typical examples in the space at our disposal.[1] If a line is drawn somewhere about 1535–40 there are something like 500 alabaster figures remaining in various states of preservation. We no longer have to describe the varied and romantic attitudes of the preceding period as all are laid flatly on their backs, mostly with hands folded in prayer. Now and then husband and wife clasp hands, as in the Earl of Warwick's tomb at Warwick (Fig. 462), and an early knight at Wantage and an almost unrecognisable fragment at Burton have the legs crossed. Knights usually rest their heads upon a tilting helm with crest (Fig. 445), and their feet on a lion or occasionally on some other beast if it is a family badge, like the bear of Warwick. Civilians and ladies usually have pillows and sometimes little angels are seated on the slab beside the cushion. Ladies almost always have dogs at their feet and often two little pet terriers are worrying the hem of their skirts. In some of the later effigies little figures of bedesmen are placed against the sole of the foot to hide the ugliness of the square-toed sabaton, as at Harewood, where the tail of the lion is twisted up over the second foot (Fig. 444). In one or two cases, as at Kinlet and Horwood, ladies have little figures of children placed in the folds of their cloaks.

The chief interest lies in the constant changes in armour and costume, which were always carefully rendered, and which must form the basis of any classification.

The earliest alabaster effigy is a knight at Hanbury, Staffs, near the quarries at Chellaston. It hardly belongs to the series as it is a typical cross-legged sword-drawing warrior of *c.* 1300 (Fig. 448).

[1] For fuller illustration the reader is referred to F. H. Crossley's splendidly illustrated *English Church Monuments*, to Stothard's drawings, and to the author's article in the *Archaeological Journal*, 1923, on "The Alabaster Tombs of the Gothic Period". *A Short History of Costume and Armour*, by F. M. Kelly and R. Schwabe, is also a useful summary of the subject.

Fig. 444. Harewood. *c.* 1490.
Fig. 446. Swine. *c.* 1420.

Fig. 445. Wingfield. *c.* 1490.
Fig. 447. Ratcliffe. *c.* 1535.

Fig. 448. Hanbury, Staffs. Earliest alabaster effigy. *c.* 1300.
Fig. 449. Gloucester. King Edward II. d. 1327.
Fig. 450. Westminster. Prince John of Eltham. d. 1334.
Fig. 451. York. Prince William of Hatfield. d. *c.* 1346.
Fig. 452. Tewkesbury. Sir Hugh Despenser. d. 1349.

Fig. 453. Gloucester. Edward II. d. 1327.

It must have been made in the ordinary way by the local carvers from the local material. The first real initiation of the alabaster trade must be traced to the royal tombs of the first half of Edward III's reign; those of his father Edward II, d. 1327; his brother John of Eltham, Earl of Cornwall, d. 1334; his young son William of Hatfield, d. c. 1346 (Figs. 449, 450, 451); and the later one of two infant children of the queen, at Westminster, William and Blanche, for which John Orchard was paid 20 shillings.

Edward II's effigy at Gloucester lies under a magnificent canopy of freestone on a Purbeck marble tomb, and this mixed use of material suggests the work of the royal masons from Westminster. It follows the type of the bronze Henry III, and has the little Westminster angels supporting the cushion. The face is of an ideal type rather than an accurate portrait, and is strikingly beautiful (Fig. 453). The Earl of Cornwall's effigy at Westminster (Fig. 450) also had a fine canopy now destroyed, and the charming little weepers of the

Fig. 454. Tewkesbury. "Sir Hugh Despenser." *c.* 1350.

tomb-chest have already been described (Fig. 275). The prince lies
with crossed legs in the easy manner of the earlier Westminster effigies.
His armour is of mixed mail and plate, and he wears the short-fronted
surcoat. Prince William of Hatfield at York (Fig. 451) is represented as
a young boy in a richly embroidered tunic and fringed cloak. An early
figure of a knight may be found in the Sir Hugh Despenser, d. 1349,
at Tewkesbury (Fig. 454). The round-topped bascinet is worn with
the camail and jupon then coming into fashion.

Ecclesiastic vestments were stereotyped, and changes were merely
in treatment and detail. The earlier bishops are perhaps more refined;
Archbishop Stratford, for instance, at Canterbury, d. 1348, is delicately rendered with an ascetic face and elaborate details of the

Fig. 455. Canterbury. Head of Archbishop Stratford. *c.* 1350.

vestments (Fig. 455). Bishop Ralph of Wells, d. 1363, is still a refined figure, but there is an increasing dryness in the handling of the drapery (Fig. 459). Bishops of *c.* 1400 have bigger heads and fuller features, and seem to lose the ascetic look of their predecessors. We may instance Archbishop Courtenay at Canterbury, d. 1396 (Fig. 456), or the splendid figure of William of Wykeham, d. 1404, at Winchester (Figs. 457, 458). This last has escaped mutilation owing to the pious protection given by old members of the college he founded,

Fig. 456. Canterbury. Archbishop Courtenay. *c.* 1395.

359

Fig. 457. Winchester. William of Wykeham. d. 1404.
Fig. 458. Winchester. William of Wykeham. Clerks at feet of effigy.

Fig. 459. Wells. Alabaster effigy of Bishop Ralph. *c.* 1360.

Fig. 460. Chichester. Alabaster effigy of Bishop Shirburne. *c.* 1535.

and as much of the colouring survives may give us a better idea of the gorgeous effect of these alabaster figures than most others. At his feet are seated three charming little figures of clerks, whose striking features mark them out as masterpieces of early fifteenth-century sculpture.

Later ecclesiastics, like Bishop Shirburne of Chichester, d. 1536 (Fig. 460), are bold and perhaps rather more florid figures, raised well above the slab. Bishop Shirburne has been repainted and is possibly touched up in other ways, but is an imposing figure, and may serve to give a better notion of what these effigies were meant to look like than more dilapidated, if more genuine examples.

A few priests occur without mitres, and in some cases wear the choir habit instead of mass vestments. The figure called William Canynge, a great merchant who took orders at the end of his life, in the church of St Mary Redcliffe, Bristol, is a striking example of this kind. The clean-cut features and bald forehead suggest a portrait (Fig. 461), but it must be pointed out that the features of a judge at Yatton, not far away, bear a strong resemblance to our Bristol priest, and the type may only be a model adopted in a common workshop.

The knights and ladies may be roughly divided into four categories, the main distinctions being governed by the changes of fashion in the armour of the men and head-dresses of the women. The four periods may be called the Edwardian, Lancastrian, Yorkist and Tudor, though there are, of course, transitional examples between each. These titles may not be strictly accurate, as the Edwardian lasts on into the reign of Henry IV, but they have the advantage of being simple and easy to remember.

(1) *The Edwardian, c.* 1350–1420

This is sometimes called the camail and jupon period, from the characteristic military accoutrements. The style has already been described in the bronze effigy of the Black Prince; a pointed steel bascinet with

Fig. 461. Bristol. St Mary Redcliffe. Alabaster effigy of ecclesiastic. c. 1490.

Fig. 462. Warwick. Alabaster effigy of Thomas Beaucharp Earl of Warwick. d. 1371.

Fig. 463. East Harling. "Nebuly" head-dress. *c.* 1375.

Fig. 464. East Harling. Camail. *c.* 1375.

the camail,[1] or curtain of mail, hanging from it to protect the neck is the characteristic feature. The jupon is a tight-fitting sleeveless garment coming down to the hips, and apparently made of leather worn over the mail shirt. It usually ends at the bottom in a scalloped fringe and is often decorated with armorial bearings. An elaborate sword-belt is worn low on the hips, and arms and legs are protected by plate. In the later examples, usually after 1400, the jupon appears to be swelling out as though worn over a steel breastplate, and the bascinet is surrounded by a jewelled circlet, called an orle, which is a very decorative feature.

The ladies wear the framed, or "nebuly", head-dress, composed of closely placed frills and either square or round, with a plain cap

[1] Called "aventail" in old English, but the French "camail" has been so widely adopted that it is retained here.

Fig. 465. Swine. *c.* 1370.   Fig. 467. Staindrop. *c.* 1425.
Fig. 466. Swine. *c.* 1420.   Fig. 468. Harewood. *c.* 1430.

behind. The camail of the knight and framed head-dress of the lady can best be seen by turning to our illustrations from East Harling in Norfolk (Figs. 463, 464). The complete figures may be illustrated by the Earl of Warwick, d. 1371 (Fig. 462), or from the earlier of the tombs at Swine (Fig. 465). In this last the lady has a simple veil over her head with a "barbe" of thin material over her chin, indicating that she was a widow, having survived her lord. A tight bodice, usually in the shape known as the sideless cote-hardie, is the regular dress with large buttons down the front and cloak thrown well back or even omitted altogether. In the later examples, after 1400, the framed head-dress begins to give way to something more akin to the elaborate convention of the next period. The hair is confined in a "crespine" or jewelled net and bunched over the ears in what are called "cauls", which are joined by a straight band, also jewelled, across the forehead. For convenience we may call this the "crespine" head-dress, though there may not be much authority for this use of the term. A good example of it in its earlier and more moderate shape may be found in Lady Mainwaring at Over Peover, Cheshire, c. 1410 (Fig. 471). She also wears the "houppelande", a cloak with a high collar introduced from Burgundy,[1] and also some-times worn by men, and about her neck is the famous SS collar, the badge of the Lancastrians, the exact meaning and derivation of which is still a matter of controversy.[2]

Later types of the camail and jupon armour may be seen in another knight at Swine (Figs. 435, 466) and in the great tomb of Ralph Nevill Earl of Westmorland, d. 1425, at Staindrop, where he lies between his two wives (Fig. 467). Unless this effigy was made a few years before his death his armour is not quite up-to-date, as the camail was by this time beginning to be abandoned. He has the

[1] There is a very similar effigy at Northleigh, near Oxford, and both knight and lady are so much alike in both places that the two must have come from the same workshop—probably in Nottingham.

[2] The earliest noted instance of this is the effigy of Sir John Swinford at Spratton, who died in 1371. He seems to have been a follower of John of Gaunt.

Fig. 469. London. St Helen's Church. "John Oteswich and wife." c. 1400.

Fig. 470. Dennington, Suffolk. "Lord Bardolf." d. 1441.

latest type of bascinet with a rich orle, and his wives have the earliest form of crespine head-dress; all three wear the SS collar.

Wealthy merchants, besides the old nobility, begin at this time to be commemorated by elaborate tombs and we find Sir William de la Pole, d. 1367, in Holy Trinity Church, Hull, represented in a long gown, beside his wife who wears a veil stretched over a square frame. He was the founder of the family which married into royal circles with disastrous results to his descendants. There is also the tomb of John Oteswich, *c.* 1400, in St Helen's Church, London. He wears the houppelande with a high collar, and a large purse or scrip at his side (Fig. 469). He has a short beard and his facial features

Fig. 471. Over Peover.
"Lady Mainwaring."
c. 1420.

Fig. 472. Arundel.
"Countess of Arundel."
c. 1420.

follow the type of the earlier Edward II. His wife has the sideless cote-hardie with buttons down the front and a simple veil over her head.

(2) *The Lancastrian, c.* 1415–50

About the time of the battle of Agincourt the mixed type of armour goes out and knights appear in full plate.[1] The camail is replaced by a gorget of plate and the jupon disappears; instead a cuirass or breast-plate is worn and the thighs are protected by a series of overlapping plates called a "fauld" or skirt of lames. A slanting "bawdrick", or sword belt, is used and the ornamental horizontal one appears to be used only to support the dagger. The orle is usually a very striking feature, and the front of the bascinet is sometimes inscribed with the sacred monogram IHS. Small plates called "tassets" or "taces" are buckled on to the lowest lame, and more elaborate elbow cops and shoulder plates are added. Ladies bring their cloaks more over the shoulder and support them by cords and richly carved brooches. The crespine head-dress becomes more elaborate and more widely extended with a wealth of jewellers' work, as at Methley (Fig. 477) or Canterbury (Fig. 476). The most elaborate of these erections is worn by the Countess of Arundel (Fig. 472), who has widespread cauls and a splendid coronet perched on the top with a veil stretched out on wires to a great distance, anticipating the butterfly head-dress of the next period. Towards the middle of the century the cauls instead of being spread widely are brought up to two points above the head, forming the horned, or mitred head-dress of which we have an example at Dennington (Fig. 470).

The Green tomb at Lowick, of which we know the sculptors, may be taken as an early example of this type (Figs. 6, 473). Ralph Green, d. 1419, holds his wife's hand and there is a canopy, referred to as a "gablette" in the contract, over their heads. Another early

[1] Several big works have been published on armour. Perhaps the most convenient handbook at a reasonable price is C. ffoulkes' *Armour and Weapons*, 1909. Kelly and Schwabe, *History of Costume and Armour*, is more up-to-date.

Fig. 473. Lowick. Ralph Green. d. 1419.
Fig. 474. Tong. Sir Richard Vernon. d. 1451.

Fig. 475. Canterbury. Head of Henry IV. d. 1413.

pair may be found at Harewood (Fig. 468) where there is one of the finest collections of well-preserved alabaster tombs in the country. Later examples are Lord Bardolf, d. 1441, at Dennington (Fig. 470) and Sir Richard Vernon, d. 1451, at Tong (Fig. 474). These last are among the most imposing of the whole series and must rank high as specimens of fifteenth-century sculpture. They wear the SS collar, and Lord Bardolf also wears the Garter strapped round below his left knee. A comparison between the Lowick and Tong figures shows the advance made in the scientific construction of the plates protecting shoulder and elbow.

One magnificent royal tomb belongs to this series, that of Henry IV and his queen Joan at Canterbury (Figs. 475, 476). The jewels of the crowns, the splendid clasps of the mantles and richly carved borders of the royal robes are finely worked, and display the suitability of the material for elaborate detail. The king has a short beard, but his hair is short and worn in a kind of roll, while his cheeks and

Fig. 476. Canterbury. "Queen Joan."   Fig. 477. Methley. "Lady Waterton."

the back of his head up to above the ears are shaven. Henry V seems
to have been clean shaven and wore his hair short, and beards become very rare after his time until they were re-introduced by
Henry VIII. Henry IV certainly gives the impression of being a
portrait; the "gablettes" over his head remind us of those of the
Earl of Arundel and of the Green monument at Lowick, so that it
is tempting to regard this group as all being the work of the Chellaston firm of Prentys and Sutton.

An interesting civilian tomb of this period is that of Chief Justice
Sir William Gascoigne, d. 1419, at Harewood (Fig. 436). He was
described by Shakespeare as the judge who dared to commit Henry V,
when Prince of Wales, for unruly conduct, and was afterwards pro-

moted by Henry as one who would administer justice without fear or favour. He wears the judge's coif, which was originally painted red, and his lady shows a good example of the crespine head-dress.

(3) *The Yorkist, c.* 1440–85

As explained already the dynastic names are used here somewhat loosely. Edward IV did not gain the throne till 1461, but though the most characteristic specimens of what we are calling Yorkist armour may be dated *c.* 1460–80 the changes began rather earlier. It is a remarkable thing that before 1440 the bare-headed warrior is practically unknown, but after 1455 the helmeted knight is almost equally rare. The head still rests on the tilting helm, but the bascinet disappears, and the four or five helmeted knights wear the "sallet", a light fighting helmet with a back projection, resembling the shape of a fisherman's sou'wester. In all other instances the head is bare, and the hair is worn short, frequently cut above the ears in what has been termed a "bowl crop", as at Dodford (Fig. 478). The armour assumes most elaborate and ornate forms with flutings and ridges designed to turn away the point of a lance; elbow and knee cops develop large wings and are laced on with carefully wrought straps and the gorget is replaced by a mail collar called the "standard of mail". Tassets become long and pointed, and the whole effect is

Fig. 478. Dodford (Northants). Alabaster effigy of Sir John Cressy. d. 1444.

Fig. 479. Salisbury. Alabaster effigy of Lord Hungerford. c. 1460.

Fig. 480. Stanton Harcourt. Sir Robert Harcourt, K.G. d. 1471.

extremely rich and varied. Ladies begin by wearing the horned head-dress, but the horns were soon brought more together and lengthened by a sort of wire framework, over which a veil was thrown, forming the famous "butterfly" head-dress. As the fluttering veil could not be easily rendered in a recumbent figure these are usually more moderately rendered in the effigies than in the brasses. In some cases a broad turned-up flap covers the front of the receding horns, and sometimes a kind of truncated pyramid replaces the horns, though the tall steeple caps shown in the manuscripts never occur on the tombs, being perhaps more a French than an English fashion. Towards the end of the period ladies sometimes wear the hair long and loose with a coronet or something like the knightly orle round the brow. The Yorkist collar of suns and roses replaces the Lancastrian SS collar after 1461.

Sir John Cressy at Dodford, d. 1444 (Fig. 478), may be taken as one of the earlier examples of the type, and Lord Hungerford, d. 1459, at Salisbury (Fig. 479), as a more typical example of the

Fig. 481. Ewelme. Head of Duchess of Suffolk. d. 1477.

elaboration of detail described above. In the later examples the hair is worn a little longer, as in the effigy of Sir Robert Harcourt, d. 1471, at Stanton Harcourt (Fig. 480). He wears the Yorkist collar and Garter robes over his armour, and his lady, who was one of the few women to belong to the order, wears the Garter on her left arm. She is represented as a widow in veil and barbe.

We have no royal effigy of this period, but the tomb of the Duchess of Suffolk, d. 1477, at Ewelme (Fig. 481), may serve as a satisfactory substitute. We have already illustrated her weepers (see Fig. 441), and now show the wan face of the Duchess in a coronet over her widow's weeds. She also wears the Garter on her left wrist. She was granddaughter of the poet Chaucer and widow of the unfortunate Duke whose murder at sea is told in the Paston Letters.

(4) *The Tudor, c.* 1485–1540

During our last period workmanship becomes uneven, especially during the latter part of the fifteenth century. As we found in the case of the architectural sculpture first-class work was available for those who could pay for it, but some of the effigies were decidedly poor. The more fantastic and florid features of the Yorkist armour disappear, and a smoother, more workmanlike effect, was sought. Tassets become larger, and in the latter part of the period huge shoulder-guards make their appearance. The "sabatons", or shoes protected by laminated steel plates, which hitherto had been pointed become blunted and square-toed (Figs. 446, 447), and sometimes little bedesmen are carved seated against the sole of the foot. The SS collar is re-introduced and hangs down lower over the breast, and the "tabard", a kind of heraldic apron, is not unfrequently worn over the armour. Hair is worn longer, down to the shoulders, and in the sixteenth century is usually cut straight across the forehead and the back of the neck, like the "bobbed hair" of little girls of to-day. Ladies, especially after 1500, wear what is known as the "pedimental" head-dress,

Fig. 482. Harewood. Sir Richard Redman. *c.* 1490.

Fig. 483. Holme Pierrepont. Sir Henry Pierrepont. d. 1499.

which is shaped like a gable with a point in the middle. At first it has long side-pieces, but later these are cut off below the ears. Loose hair with coronets or the orle-like circlet are still found sometimes, and widows still have the veil and barbe. The flapped caps are still used at the beginning of the period.

These details are more clearly brought out by a reference to the illustrations than by description. Sir Richard Redman at Harewood (Fig. 482) is a well-preserved and very pleasing figure of the end of the century. He wears the Tudor collar combining the Lancastrian SS with the Yorkist roses. Lady Redman looks modest in her widow's weeds. The little bedesman sitting on the lion against Sir Richard's foot has already been illustrated (see Fig. 444). Another well-preserved knight of this period at Holme Pierrepont (Fig. 483) is identified as Sir Henry Pierrepont, d. 1499, though he still wears the Yorkist

378

Fig. 484. Ratcliffe-on-Soar. Ralph Sacheverell. d. 1539.

collar. The armour, however, is of the later type. The tomb of Ralph
Sacheverell, d. 1539, at Ratcliffe-on-Soar, is also typical of the last
phase of Gothic armour. He has the bobbed hair, high shoulder-
guard and drooping SS collar, while his wife wears the pedimental
head-dress (Fig. 484).

The monument of Sir Richard Knightley, d. 1534, at Fawsley
(Fig. 485), is perhaps the most imposing of the later tombs. It is
perfectly preserved and retains much of the original colour. Sir
Richard wears a very ornate specimen of the heraldic tabard, and
the quilted sleeves of his lady are the first sign of the coming change
of costume which was carried to such extremes under Elizabeth.
Certain details common to this and to the fine late tombs at Alder-
maston and Windsor distinguish this group from the regular Nottingham type exemplified by the Ratcliffe figures. Possibly they were
London productions.

Fig. 485. Fawsley. Sir Richard Knightley. d. 1534.

Fig. 486. Holbeach. Freestone Knight. *c.* 1360.

The *freestone effigies* of the fourteenth and fifteenth centuries need
not detain us long. They followed the fashions of the alabaster models
with a necessary coarsening due to the rougher material, and seldom
introduced any new features of their own. A fine knight of *c.* 1360
at Holbeach, Lincs (Fig. 486), proves that the Ancaster masons still
retained something of their pristine skill, and could produce tombs
of distinction; and at Bristol, where the oolite masons had managed
to compete with the Purbeck marblers in the thirteenth century, the
effigy of Abbot Newbury, *c.* 1475 (Fig. 487), shows that their fine-
grained stone was capable of detail which could be set beside that
of the alabaster-men. Elsewhere, however, the stone effigies are
mainly copies of the alabasters, and one has only to look at such a
figure as we show from Gaddesby (Fig. 489) to see its close resemblance
to the late alabaster knights like the Sacheverell at Ratcliffe-on-Soar.
The wooden effigies of the Earl and Countess of Westmorland at
Brancepeth follow the alabaster types so closely that it has been

Fig. 487. Bristol. Lady Chapel. Freestone memorial of Abbot Newbury. *c.* 1475.

Fig. 488. Brancepeth, Durham. Wooden memorial of Second Earl of Westmorland and Countess. *c.* 1484.
The accoutrement of the Knight is that of *c.* 1450.

Fig. 489. Gaddesby. Stone copy of alabaster model. *c.* 1520.

Fig. 490. St David's (South Wales). End of tomb-chest. *c.* 1500.

suggested that these were the patterns submitted by the tomb-makers for approval before reproducing them in the more expensive material (Fig. 488). The weepers also follow the alabaster patterns, but it is worth while to illustrate a fine Resurrection (Fig. 490) from the tomb of Bishop Morgan, d. 1504, at St David's, which exhibits a liveliness of action outside the stock models. This is possibly due to suggestions coming from the Flemish tomb-makers, whose productions were introduced into England on a large scale in the following generation.

This has necessarily had to be a somewhat sketchy description of the monumental trade which provided such a large proportion of our late Gothic sculptures. It was found convenient to fix a limit to our studies of the architectural sculpture at about 1535–40, by which time the monasteries had been suppressed and images removed from the churches. For many years tombs in alabaster and other materials continued to be made which retained much of the Gothic feeling, even if combined with Renaissance details.[1] The fine effigy of the Earl of Huntingdon, d. 1561, at Ashby-de-la-Zouch, might for instance have passed for a much earlier figure if it had not been for his long beard. A line must, however, be drawn somewhere, and the Reformation is probably the most distinctive point at which it can be fixed.

[1] These have been ably dealt with by J. G. Mann in an article on "English Church Monuments, 1536–1625", published in the Walpole Society's 21st volume, 1932–3.

SELECTED BIBLIOGRAPHY

E. S. PRIOR and A. GARDNER. *Medieval Figure Sculpture in England.*

S. GARDNER. *English Gothic Foliage Sculpture.*

A. W. CLAPHAM. *English Romanesque Architecture before the Conquest.*
—— *English Romanesque Architecture after the Conquest.*
BALDWIN BROWN. *The Arts in Early England.*
W. G. COLLINGWOOD. *Northumbrian Crosses of the Pre-Norman Age.*
J. BRØNDSTED. *Early English Ornament.*

M. D. ANDERSON. *The Medieval Carver.*
M. H. LONGHURST. *English Ivories.*
C. E. KEYSER. *Norman Tympana and Lintels.*
J. ROMILLY ALLEN. *Christian Symbolism in Great Britain and Ireland.*
W. R. LETHABY. *Mediaeval Art.*
—— *Westminster Abbey and the King's Craftsmen.*
— *Westminster Abbey Re-examined.*
F. E. HOWARD and F. H. CROSSLEY. *English Church Woodwork.*
F. H. CROSSLEY. *English Church Monuments.*
C. A. STOTHARD. *Monumental Effigies of Great Britain.*
A. C. FRYER. *Wooden Monumental Effigies.*
F. M. KELLY and R. SCHWABE. *A Short History of Costume and Armour.*
F. BOND. *Fonts and Font-covers.*
—— *Wood-carvings in English Churches:* (1) *Misericords.*
—— *Wood-carvings in English Churches:* (2) *Stalls.*
The volumes published by the Royal Commission on Ancient Monuments, especially *London—Westminster Abbey.*
The Little County Guides.
Various papers in journals of learned Societies, mostly referred to in the notes, the most important being: Sir W. St J. Hope and W. R. Lethaby, "The Imagery and Sculptures on the West Front of Wells Cathedral Church", *Archaeologia*, LIX, 1904; Sir W. St J. Hope, "On the Early Working of Alabaster in England", *Archaeological Journal*, 1904; A. Gardner, "Alabaster Tombs of the Gothic Period", *Archaeological Journal*, 1923; P. B. Chatwin, "Monumental Effigies in Warwickshire", *Transactions Birmingham Archaeological Society*, 1921, 1922, 1923; F. H. Crossley, "Mediaeval Monumental Effigies remaining in Cheshire", *Transactions Historic Society of Lancs and Cheshire*, 1925, etc.
Local Guides and Monographs.

SELECTED BIBLIOGRAPHY

A. GARDNER. *Medieval Sculpture in France.*

A. MICHEL. *Histoire de l'Art.*

L. LEFRANÇOIS PILLION. *Les Sculpteurs Français du XIIe Siècle.*

—— *Les Sculpteurs Français du XIIIe Siècle.*

M. AUBERT. *La Sculpture Française du Moyen Age et de la Renaissance.*

E. MÂLE. *L'Art Religieuse du XIIe Siècle en France.*

—— *L'Art Religieuse du XIIIe Siècle en France.*

—— *L'Art Religieuse de la Fin du Moyen Age en France.*

    Etc., etc.

INDEX OF PERSONS

387

INDEX OF PLACES

(Illustrations on pages in darker type)

INDEX OF PLACES

CAMBRIDGE : PRINTED BY W. LEWIS, M.A., AT THE UNIVERSITY PRESS